REACHING YOUTH TODAY:
HEIRS TO THE WHIRLWIND

REACHING YOUTH TODAY:
HEIRS TO THE WHIRLWIND

Barbara Hargrove
Stephen D. Jones

JUDSON PRESS ® VALLEY FORGE

The material on which this book is based was presented under the auspices of the Boardman Lectureship at the American Baptist Assembly, Green Lake, Wisconsin.

Scripture quotations in this book are taken from the following versions of the Bible:

The New English Bible. Copyright © The Delegates of the Oxford University Press and the Syndics of the Cambridge University Press 1961, 1970.

Revised Standard Version of the Bible copyrighted 1946, 1952 © 1971, 1973 by the Division of Christian Education of the National Council of the Churches of Christ in the U.S.A., and used by permission.

Good News Bible, the Bible in Today's English Version. Copyright © American Bible Society, 1976. Used by permission.

The Jerusalem Bible, copyright © 1966 by Darton, Longman & Todd, Ltd. and Doubleday and Company, Inc. Used by permission of the publisher.

Library of Congress Cataloging in Publication Data

Hargrove, Barbara.
   Reaching youth today.
   Includes bibliographical references.
   1. Youth—United States—Religious life.
2. Church work with youth—United States.
3. Youth—United States. I. Jones, Stephen D.
II. Title.
BV4531.2.H33 1983   261.8'342   83–100
ISBN 0-8170-0977-9

Contents

Introduction *9*

1 Heirs to the Whirlwind *13*

2 Work and Entitlement in a Postindustrial Society *31*

3 Seeking the Self in a Consumer Society *47*

4 Youth and the Public Dimension *63*

5 Courageous Evangelism *83*

6 Conversion Without End *93*

7 Culture-Shaping Evangelism *105*

8 God's Time—The Right Time *115*

Notes *123*

66739

REACHING YOUTH TODAY:
HEIRS TO THE WHIRLWIND

Introduction

The first portion of this book is a discussion of *youth and culture*. The praise of youth has always been a value of civilization. From Ponce de León's search for the fountain of youth to the fairy-tale classic, Peter Pan, we see that a societal norm is to be young or youthful.

It is not difficult to observe around us the multitude of young celebrities. Youth are admired by all ages of our population. Children wish to be older; adults wish to be younger. The value of being youthful has led businesses to exploit youth for their own gain.

Although society values youthfulness, young people themselves are frequently misunderstood and discriminated against. Youth are *used* rather than respected as participating members of society. A recent study in Florida reveals that when youth and older adults are arrested for the same crime, the older adult is often excused and sent to a rehabilitation facility and the youth is sent to jail.

As youth begin to formulate their value systems, they are very much subject to the influence of their peers. The similarity in the appearance of youth stems from their basic need for identity and not from the generalization that "youth are all alike." However, a New Jersey town recently passed a town ordinance that forbids any youth, regardless of who the youth is or what purpose he or she has, to be out on the streets past a night curfew hour. Such a blanket treatment of youth shows a naive understanding of the young person and disrespect of individual rights.

The role that we give youth in our society is contradictory. The voices of our younger citizenry are almost absent when decisions about them and their welfare are made, but their bodies are considered old enough to die in war.

The second part of this book is about *youth evangelism*. The place of youth in the church has been a topic of discussion for some time. For a large part, youth have had a difficult time discovering a role which they and the larger church community can mutually affirm to be legitimate. At times, the roles that the youth of the church have wanted have not been open to them. At other times, the roles which the church has wanted them to fill have been exploitative and demeaning.

This lack of clear and accurate communication has given youth mixed signals on whether or not the church wants any part of them. It has also made the church "gun-shy" and afraid to explore new ways to minister for and with youth.

The church today is facing, in many denominations, a survival problem. Declining worship attendance and church school enrollment have alarmed church leaders and stimulated them to begin exploring new ways of reaching new people. A recent census revealed that one million persons become adolescents each year. How can the church begin reaching more of today's youth? The subject of youth evangelism now has become a crucial concern, particularly for youth ministry professionals.

However, before an effective evangelistic thrust can be launched, the planners, the writers, the implementers, the parents, and everyone who ministers with and for youth must fully understand how the younger person acquires faith. Not taking the time to understand recent research in this area only leads us to mirror the past and try to guess what might work. Such an approach can, at best, reinforce current confusion and, at worst, result in new negative experiences between youth and the church.

The questions posed by these two topics, *Youth and Culture* and *Youth Evangelism,* are facing youth ministry professionals today. How do we understand the relationship of youth and culture? What then are our roles as concerned adults who work with youth? How do youth acquire faith? What are ways in which adults and the church can begin to evangelize youth?

In November of 1981 a group of youth-ministry professionals gathered at Green Lake, Wisconsin, to begin to work on these questions. The conference, called "Creation 2," was sponsored by the Department of Ministry with Youth of the American Baptist

Churches in the U.S.A. To begin exploring these issues, participants listened to, interacted with, and were challenged by two resource lecturers—Barbara Hargrove and Stephen Jones. Barbara, a professor of the sociology of religion, helped the participants to understand the interrelatedness of recent generations and the effects that cultural norms in such areas as work ethics and consumerism have on persons today. She also discussed the role of youth in relationship to the public dimension of life. Steve, a local church pastor, presented insights on the important role of adults as "courageous evangelists" with youth and the task of the church in nurturing the faith of youth.

The two series of lectures, although originating from two perspectives, became interwoven when Barbara spoke about the need for churches to function as "mediating structures" in our society in order to help youth gain a responsible identity and when Steve spoke about "culture-shaping evangelism," the call to evangelize our society to be more Christlike and Christ-centered. In both of these presentations the lecturers stimulated participants to begin to look seriously at these issues and offered helpful insights in response to the challenges they generate.

The lectures, with the editing assistance of Wendell Brooker, a participant at the conference and a writer and youth ministry professional, are in this book. When you read the lectures, you will find, as did the participants at the conference, an understanding of the culture and world in which we live and some ways in which we can begin to reach today's youth.

This book is not intended to be conclusive on the topics of youth and culture and youth evangelism. But rather, it is presented to begin the process of thinking, exploring, and perhaps evolving some answers that will enable our ministry with youth to be more effective. As an aid to this process, questions for reflection have been appended to each chapter.

The world we live in is a complicated one. The simple answers we would like to have are not to be found. By confronting the issues in this book, we are beginning to sharpen our own understanding and skills in order to minister to, with, and for youth.

Donald Ng
Department of Ministry with Youth
American Baptist Churches in the U.S.A.

1
Heirs to the Whirlwind

Youth today stand in a unique place in the history of American society; they live among people whose character and ways of perceiving life were formed in very different ways from their own.

If we could listen in on an intergenerational conversation among members of the youth generations of the '40s, '60s, and '80s, we would hear the clash of very distinctive perceptions. For example, if they were considering a relatively simple question such as "What is something that you need?" their responses would be disconcertingly different. If the answers were (1) "I need to help put meat on the table," (2) "I need to find a draft deferment," and (3) "I need to buy a new videocassette player," it would be easy to place the answers with the proper generation. Can people with such different perceptions of need genuinely talk with one another? The obvious answer indicates the source of much of our intergenerational tension. The problem is intensified when the questions become more complex. Consider, for example, potential responses to questions like "What do you mean when you say things are going well?" or "How do you distinguish between good and evil?"

We realize that there are people still active in our society who were shaped by a culture that in comparison with the present seems static, called upon as it was to survive the Great Depression. There are people whose formative years were spent during the great population shifts and technological revolution that accompanied World War II. There are people now entering the age brackets of the "command generation," those who were caught up in the rebellion against what the post-World-War-II society had become. In the ways most relevant to a person's sense of self and place in society, all those people grew up in cultures alien to that of today's youth.

Generations in a family are easy to trace. In a society, defining the generations becomes more complicated since biological generations overlap and become blurred. The mark of a sociological generation, says Karl Mannheim, is a particular event, or series of events, that affects the perception of the world by the people who have gone through the experience. At the same time, the effect on different participants will vary according to the perceptual filter provided by a particular person's previous experience. Those who are growing up at the time of such an influential event will have their perceptual filters determined by it to some extent. It will become the norm by which all succeeding experiences will be interpreted.[1] For that reason, in order to know the human environment in which today's youth live, it may be helpful to review some of the shaping experiences of recognizable sociological generations in our time. This will be done with broad strokes, masking the complexity and concentrating on the experience of the white middle class because of the way their experience has been understood as the norm in our society.

World War II: The Generational Experience of Youth in the Great Cultural Shift

No one living in the decade before World War II would have called the time static. It was a period of change, confusion, and insecurity. After a period of unbridled optimism based largely on the commercial expansion of the nation, people had been plunged into despair, watching the collapse of the economy that was the source of their hope. Hardworking and able people were suddenly unemployed and forced to seek assistance of a type they had been taught to regard as demeaning. Fighting for prices and wages and jobs that would keep them from such a fate, labor unions became militant. Farmers (good old, reliable farmers!) organized and dumped milk on the ground rather than sell it at impossible prices. Business leaders regrouped and sought new ways of coping. Seeking to stabilize the economy, the government closed the banks, but in doing so, reinforced the feeling that institutions were becoming untrustworthy. Then it instituted the programs of the New Deal, which began to correct some of the most glaring problems of the depression. The price of this government correction, however, was a disturbance of the people's understanding of the nature and function of their social institutions. The public order itself seemed threatened. It was not a placid time.

As the sharper traumas of the depression began to recede, they were replaced by anxieties about international affairs. People read their newspapers and listened to their radios with horror as they watched the rise of Hitler in Germany and the rape of successive nations by an apparently invincible Nazi force. The Spanish Civil War and Mussolini's adventurism in Ethiopia added to the feeling that chaos would be the result of any attempt to be involved in international affairs. Isolationism became impossible as the progression of events in Europe seemed to be drawing the United States inevitably into the maelstrom. It was not a placid time.

Yet by today's standards most people lived a settled and predictable existence. Even dislocated farmers escaping the dust bowl were able to find the fertile valleys of California and a chance to start again. For the majority of the population, the fight against poverty and chaos took place within the bounds of neighborhoods and social groups where common values were taken for granted and where social support was a tradition. In fact, the pressing needs of the time tended to increase the level of mutual aid and the strength of the bonds within family, neighborhood, occupational, and church groups. Tight budgets kept people at home more and increased the value of free neighborhood recreational activities. Church and charitable groups provided important services. As the ability to make monetary contributions to them dwindled, the willingness to offer volunteer service often increased. In this way the level of sociability and involvement increased. Such groups then became, for some people, substitutes for more widely based action.

In comparison with their immediate past, those years brought many people closer to others of similar circumstances and backgrounds, but farther from groups and classes different from themselves. Travel was curtailed; risks were closer to home. The values and life-styles passed on to children had little competition. It was relatively easy to know what was right and what was wrong, what worked and what did not work. There were plenty of people to reinforce those standards and just enough who did not fit them to serve as examples of what not to do and be.

America was then, as it has generally been, a pluralistic society with a great diversity in life-styles and values. But most people experienced only one part of that diversity. The particular tradition and region and class in which they grew up was understood to be "American" culture. Other ways of living and other groups were treated, like the local misfits, as bad examples. Even the common pattern of bright young people escaping the smothering narrowness of "Main Street" for the big-city lights was diminished in those years; urban people were coming home to the family farm instead, seeking at least subsistence in the wreckage of a collapsed economy. The adults of that time, the most senior of today's senior citizens, may have experienced the depression years as an aberration, but for the children growing up in those years, that was the way the world was. Neighborhoods were close, money and goods were scarce, moral values were clear and simple, and good people could be expected to follow well-established patterns of behavior. Even the most urban tended to know only their "own kind." One might say that the dominant behavior pattern was that of small-town morality.

World War II cut across that picture like a sharp sword. Most of the young men of the nation were caught up into military service and were thrown into close contact for a long time with others from very different backgrounds. They discovered through countless experiences that good people could follow cultural patterns different from the one each had learned was right. They saw patterns of status overturned as the new technology of war elevated some and bypassed others with no regard for previous social standing. Veterans came home to a society willing to grant them a college education in order to train them for a culture transformed by technological changes. Rather than returning to the relatively closed communities and stable neighborhoods they had left, they moved to college campuses, often with new wives and young children. Leaving those campuses with training for occupations often unrelated to those of other members of their families of origin or the old neighborhoods, they moved to areas where they could find relevant work and settled in the fast-growing suburbs. There they were joined by people who had left their hometowns to move to the centers of the defense industry during the war and who had saved money to invest in housing when it became available. In these new surroundings free of local tradition, families set about, consciously or not, to create a culture appropriate to their new affluence. Schools, churches, and clubs sprang up out of the suburban neighborhoods to accommodate this purpose. The ways in which these people and their institutions structured their lives and value systems were taken from an eclectic search through available options. Their lives were often shaped by visions of the good life taken from the new medium of television.

The Generational Experience of Youth in the 1960s: Dislocation

The first generation of children to grow up in this newly created environment constituted the post-World-War-II baby boom. Their experiences were influenced not only by the tentativeness of the suburban culture, but also by their numbers. Overcrowded schools demanded new methods of teaching to deal with the crowding, as well as to take advantage of newly available technology. Because of the large number of these children, the focus of public attention seemed to be constantly on them. The early 1950s saw a peak in interest in books on child rearing and in movies and TV programs about families with young children. By the end of that decade, adolescence was becoming a national preoccupation. The middle and late 1960s were the years when the college campus dominated the public consciousness. In all of these periods there was the expectation that this generation of young people, these inheritors of the new life-styles, could really bring our American society into a golden future. Only they could deal comfortably with an age of high technology, rapid change, and constant sensory stimulation. Margaret Mead has said that in traditional societies, adults could directly model the future for their young; in moderately changing societies, the generations could cooperate on building the future; but in modern society the adults are aliens, needing to be led by the young.[2]

Given this expectation and subsequent self-image, young people in this period were particularly critical of the society that they heard about from their academic mentors and saw portrayed on television, which was rapidly becoming a significant source of learning about the world. The confrontation precipitated by the civil rights movement was the first active portrayal of such criticism to be carried on national television news. The gap between the actions of recalcitrant, racist governors and police and the idyllic suburban world of such fictional programs as "Leave It to Beaver" and "Father Knows Best" hit young people with particular force. It was Martin Luther King, Jr., himself, who made the connection between the civil rights movement and the war in Vietnam, just when these young people were beginning to anticipate the end of their comfortable suburban world in the jungles of that remote nation and its war. For the young, the connection with the civil rights movement helped to legitimate their opposition to the war, which on one hand they saw as an imperialist adventure and on the other hand they understood as the deliberate ploy of an antagonistic government bent on controlling and/or destroying their generation. Lacking direct channels to political means of dealing with such public issues and alienated from the styles of private life they had known, a significant portion of the youth of the 1960s revolted in one or both of two ways.

One branch of the movement was primarily concerned with the private realm and individual consciousness. Convinced that they had been taught false interpretations of the very nature of reality, they sought new visions, new ways of ordering their world. The dry scientism that had accompanied the technological emphasis of their times was found incapable of supporting a truly human life. Instead, they sought emotion and ecstasy, often with the help of hallucinogenic drugs. They dropped out of school and strove to enter a world fundamentally different from the one represented by the school. They experimented with new social forms, rejecting the patterns of morality and the expectations of a competitive life-style, which they had been taught. They left school for a life in the street and in communal "pads," where any rules or patterns were established by consensus, if at all.

The other branch of the movement was political and sought to use the techniques of demonstration and civil disobedience that had proved so effective in the civil rights movement. The effectiveness of protest was clear in such political results as the growing concern among the general population about the Vietnam war, the opening of the polls to younger voters by concerned legislatures, and the decision of the president (Lyndon Johnson) not to run for a second term in 1968. But the Kent State killings awakened young people to the price of revolution, and only the most determined—and most extreme—remained in later revolutionary cadres.

Both processes, however, had worked to drive a wedge between the young and the rest of the society. Among the young the attitude was "Don't trust anyone over thirty!" Older people, on the other hand, assumed that all young people, or at least those who adopted some of the clothing and hairstyles of the movement, were dangerous revolutionaries and drug addicts. The greatest effect of the youth movement of the late '60s and early '70s was the alienation of that group from other generations, a division that today's youth have inherited.

At this time sociological generations were turning over with amazing speed. The next such generation would be, on the average, no more than five years younger than the protest generation of the 1960s and would often include younger members of the same household. These young people, however, had not grown up in the placid suburbs that their older brothers and sisters labeled "plastic" and shallow. Rather, their early world was chaotic, responding to the shattering forces of the social movements whirling around its edges. By the time they were old enough to notice, their families were likely to be involved, not with the task of establishing a new and better life-style to reflect affluence and mobility, but with a desperate response to the youthful rebellion of older brothers and sisters. They may have peeked in on all-night sessions of older youth or confrontations between those youth and their parents concerning bad drug trips or disclosure of drug use or illegal activism. They may have seen parents try to reclaim older siblings from jails or hospital emergency rooms. They grew up on a fare of TV news that showed assassinations of important public figures, burning of cities, riots in the streets, and continual footage from the Vietnam war. They became old enough to vote and to feel some connection with the political process just in time for the Watergate scandals to destroy any faith they may have had in political institutions. The schools they attended were torn by strife between those who tried to emulate older youth by protesting about school rules and public issues and those who felt a threat in such activities.

The majority of this new sociological generation were not interested in becoming revolutionaries. They had been too young at the inception of the protests to understand the ideologies that underlay them. They only knew the costs, some of which they had paid in their own lives. The formative experiences that shaped their perceptions of the world were not those alienating experiences with large and unfriendly institutions, but rather experiences of rapid change and instability—for some, chaos. For them, the task was not to expand their world, but to order it. They often expressed hostility toward the members of the older sociological generation, so near to them in age, who appeared to them to have created havoc in the society out of selfish motives, seeking only their own gratification and leaving the younger people to deal with the leavings.

The Generational Experience of Youth in the '80s: Heirs to the Whirlwind

Youth of the 1980s may have as teachers or other adult leaders persons who are members of all those previous generations. But their experience is not that of any of them. Daniel Yankelovich, who has traced the development of American culture over the past three decades in his book *New Rules,* says that "we have moved from an uptight culture set in a dynamic economy to a dynamic culture set in an uptight economy."[3] For today's youth that dynamic culture and uptight economy are their reality. Like their grandparents who grew up during the depression, they are at least minimally aware of the limits of economic reality. Some have experienced the direct effects of economic cutbacks on their families when their parents have lost jobs or opportunities for advancement or when the rate of inflation has brought into question new purchases or particular college choices. They experience it also in the public rhetoric concerning ecology and limits to growth. At the same time, the cultural options that were perceived by the only slightly older sociological generation as chaos are, to these youth, simply the nature of reality. The experience of living and working closely with those whose values and styles of life are very different from their own, the experience which so altered the world of their grandfathers during World War II, is their day-to-day experience in most public junior and senior high schools in the 1980s. Even in private schools, scholarship programs and deliberate racial and ethnic diversification are the rule, except in those established specifically to escape such pluralism. But even that attempt at avoidance may be futile since the very existence of these schools is evidence of still another choice among the many options available in the society.

The majority of today's youth are related to a number of reference groups, each one of which may offer a different set of values and a different way of looking at the world. At the same time, the choices they make and the groups they relate to are not in the spotlight the way youth activities were in the later 1950s and early 1960s. Population data indicate that youth in the 1980s are a much smaller proportion of the society than during the earlier period. Public attention seems to continue to focus on members of the population bulge, who have now reached their thirties. Today's youth, therefore, experience less social pressure and less social support than were common to other recent generations of youth.

In their relative obscurity, youth of today are coping with the range of options they face in a wide variety of ways. Some are unusually free and self-directed, conscious of life's ambiguities, and facing them with neither excessive naiveté nor debilitating cynicism. Others find ways out of the ambiguity, either through their own actions or those of their families. Many parents, perceiving the bewildering numbers of options and kinds of companions available to their offspring, seek to protect them from making wrong choices. They may carefully circumscribe their social life, or they may withdraw them from the more pluralistic public schools to place them in private, often religious, schools where the parents can have some confidence that a consistent point of view will be expressed and where a common set of behaviors will be expected of students. Some young people find a similar option for themselves in groups, also often religious, that provide a closed community and a rigid set of rules. Parents and others are likely to define these groups as "cults," but, in fact, they offer essentially the same sort of benefits sought by the more conservative parents. In both cases there is an attempt to control, rather than to adjust to, the wider public world, which is no longer directly touched by the increasingly private world of the family. In both cases, interestingly enough, religion is a common tool for achieving that control.

On the other hand, a large number of today's youth opt for neither acceptance nor control but, rather, for escape from the complications of the modern world. The least noticed but probably most populous segment simply drift off into a world of fiction, absorbed into a life of television-watching interspersed with as many visits to the movie theater as they can afford and with an occasional celebratory high note when show-business figures come to town for personal appearances. Typifying this approach to life is the saga of young John Hinkley, who attempted to assassinate President Ronald Reagan in order to show his love for a young movie star, borrowing the idea from one of her movies.

More widely recognized forms of escape include the use of drugs and alcohol, both of which offer a chemical gateway into a reality different from one's everyday surroundings. The way young people immerse themselves in electronic games may be evidence of another way of creating one's own world, a world governed, at least to some extent, by the level of one's skill rather than by outside forces. Between the two poles of invisibility and social problem lie many other adaptations, including the total enveloping of oneself in the music preferred in the youth culture—by defiantly carrying a blaring portable radio through a crowd of less-than-appreciative people, or by wearing the less noticeable but more isolating earphones. In all of these cases I have labeled "escapist," the reaction to the range of choices in modern society has been to create from them a private world that few can enter, in which one can both, paradoxically, be self-absorbed and lose oneself.

The Changing Family: "Haven in a Heartless World"?

What, then, of the family—that institution expected to be both private and self-affirming in our social context? Many youth of the 1980s have a family different from that which has been considered traditional in American life. They are inheritors of a cultural definition of the family as an isolated nuclear unit of parents and minor offspring. They also live in households that have followed a general trend, deviating only briefly in the post-World-War-II period, of smaller and smaller families. Family size, in recent times, has moved from an average of 3.3 persons in the household in 1960 to 2.75 in 1980. The definition of any family lacking two parents as "broken" has eroded as the percentage of single-family households has moved from 9 percent in 1960 to 14 percent in 1980. Similarly, the expectation that families will remain permanent, a solid backdrop against which youth may develop their identity, has also eroded. Nationwide, one child of every eight who lives in a two-parent family has had one parent or the other replaced through divorce or death and subsequent remarriage. Many of these are "part-time children," spending part of the year in the home of each parent, often with unrelated siblings.

Once it was expected that church families would avoid such

problems, since the social control of the church was expected to prevent divorce and remarriage, or at least lessen the number. But, in reality, this is no longer the case. By observation, if not through personal experience, today's youth know that whatever the family may be to them, it cannot be expected to be the solid, unchanging entity that earlier generations assumed and that some contemporaries desperately try to affirm.

At the same time, the function of the family in the lives of members has changed. Our urbanized culture has almost entirely removed the world of work from that of the home. Even farmers have expanded their acreage to the point that they must drive their large tractors far from the sight of the farmhouse. Commuting has become an expected part of the national life-style. While a number of corporations are experimenting with ways to humanize the workplace, most people expect the world of work to be, at best, impersonal and, at worst, hostile to the individual. The pressures of a highly competitive industrial system and of a public domain that represents a precarious balance of the interests of competing groups lead the individual to look to the home to be what Christopher Lasch has termed a "haven in a heartless world."[4] Because it is so important that this haven remain free of conflict and supportive of its members, families tend to avoid issues that might be divisive.

Discipline of the young may be rather tentative for two reasons, then. First, there is the potential conflict inherent in firm action; and second, parents are not always sure what guidance to give in a changing world. Thus, says Lasch, children are robbed of the kind of loving opposition that allows the development of strong personalities and the growth of a firm sense of identity. Studies now show that the primary source of parental influence on youth is through their internalization of family standards rather than through direct guidance.[5]

One of the primary sources of family influence, as we have noted, is in the ordering of young people's lives through the choice of schools and other basic environments. In this way parents can indirectly control the influence of the peer group, a primary force in the lives of today's youth. But while youth may have internalized parental norms as moral guides, it is still the members of their peer groups who model day-to-day the behavior through which they receive acceptance into the culture of their own generation. The place of that generation in our social structure is part of its inheritance from the Vietnam generation.

Youth Culture as an Established Institution

The nature and influence of the peer group has become an established part of the structure of modern life. One cannot say that it was invented by the protesters of the late 1960s and early 1970s because it has been growing for some time. But the movement in which they were engaged and the societal response to them as people were the catalysts that set the culture of youth apart and set it spinning off in its own direction.

As we shall see, one of the primary forces of cultural drift, which is working to make the period of youth longer and more separate from the rest of life, is the nature of work in our industrialized society. As the workplace has been removed from the home, it has become increasingly less possible for the young to enter the work force gradually, guided by their families. Rather, we have come to depend upon the educational system to provide our children with the knowledge, skills and attitudes necessary to carry on adult roles in society, first in terms of work, and later in other ways as well.

Probably the most influential acts of the American government, so far as the nature of work in our culture is concerned, were the Morrill Land Grant Act of 1862, which provided for the support of state colleges to teach and do research in practical vocational subjects and in subjects dealing with science and technology, and the Smith-Lever Act, which made permanent the extension services of those colleges, along with its parallel, the Smith-Hughes Act, which set up government support on a continuing basis for vocational programs in the nation's high schools early in this century. These programs grew out of the need for vocational training no longer available in the home. They also established the school as the appropriate agency for such training, down-playing apprenticeships and other forms of skills acquisition. In the process, they helped to build a culture that would stress the importance of secondary education, and later of higher education, for nearly all of its people, thus making the school the primary social institution in the lives of the young.

This, of course, implies that the young will spend a longer period of their lives in the role of student. It also sets up the expectation that these years will be spent in full-time schooling if possible. As a result, this period remains one of continued dependency. When the category of "student," long applied to children, began to mean adolescents and then postadolescents, it tended to trap those age groups into a status of continued childhood. Yet the groups were made up of individuals old enough, strong enough, and with sufficient biological maturity to fill adult roles in less complex cultures. Before the middle of the twentieth century, adolescence had become a social category, one often considered problematic.

"Youth" as a social category came into its own in the post-World-War-II period and usually meant a group older than that termed "adolescent." Two factors assisted this development. On one hand, the technological advances of the time demanded more sophisticated workers and promised great futures to those who could expand the scientific and technological frontiers. On the other hand, given the tentativeness of the postwar suburban culture, education became the expected source of both guiding and affirming the developing life-style. So the years in schools—and of dependency—were lengthened. These years were spent in educational institutions ever more separate from the rest of the society.

It was those who, consciously or not, pursued higher education for more general cultural purposes who formed the nucleus of the student protest and the counterculture of the late '60s and early '70s. For reasons of family status if no other, many were sent to colleges whose tradition had been the training of an elite to serve as cultural arbiters, and the mentors students encountered there denounced the narrow conformity of the American suburbs. Students at these colleges and universities, and those in liberal arts programs influenced by them and joined by some students of the social sciences who had learned of social problems through those disciplines, spearheaded the youth movements of that period. Students in more scientific, technological, and professional fields tended to be "career minded," as defined by Daniel Yankelovich, and distinct from the "postaffluent," the nascent cultural elite.[6]

When one considers the negative view of the culture developed among these elite young people and the sense of antagonism they felt toward a society apparently willing to sacrifice their generation to a war they saw no legitimate reason for entering, it is hardly surprising that they rebelled. As the rebellion gained notoriety through media attention, reaction from the rest of the society tended to be strong and negative. The government now felt threatened from within, as well as from without, and so began to define these youthful rebels as enemies of the state.

Youth, sensing the growing chasm between themselves and the rest of society, began to seek solidarity through symbolic life-styles and behavior, even if they were not actively involved in rebellion in the political sphere. After a decade or more of military-style crew cuts, young men began letting their hair and beards grow. Scorning the "Ivy League" look of the '50s, young people adopted clothing styles of the poor—old jeans, torn sweatshirts, dresses pulled out of charity barrels of used clothing or off the racks of stores that served the underclasses of the society. Music, already a mark of different age groups, became for these youth a form of protest. The lyrics were often political or cultural statements about the society, but they were often masked by the even stronger protest of the beat and the volume of an electronic musical style that adults, on the whole, could not stand.

But more than symbols and styles were involved. The content of the lives of these youth was a direct protest against what they saw as the "establishment." They dropped out of the schools that were to have prepared them for adult roles in the larger society. They dropped out of patterns of dating and mate selection that were to have prepared them for future family roles, choosing instead communal life-styles and uninhibited sex. They dropped out of expected patterns of consumption in nearly all areas except those related to their music, shunning shoes and household gadgets, experimenting with diets, or subsisting on begged or discarded food. They deserted both the primary religious institutions of the society and the "faith" of the secular universities, seeking new visions in hallucinogenic drugs and techniques of meditation borrowed from Eastern religions. Or they took up various political faiths and sought a revolution, one that would allow their movement to support the movements of less-privileged people.

The combination of cultural and political threats created a defensive reaction in the wider society, which reinforced the sense of distance between that social milieu and the young. Each reaction increased the solidarity of the youthful rebels, so that by the time of the shooting by the National Guard of four student demonstrators at Kent State, the break between the youth culture and its host society seemed clear and wide.

The significance of the Kent State tragedy, as compared with the impact of the almost simultaneous shooting of black youth at Jackson State, is evidence of the grounding of the youth culture in the American white middle class and a source of some of the cynicism of the following generation. While black protest sometimes accompanied white student movements, it was symbolic, except among the more dedicated revolutionaries, of the desire of black youth to become part of the very vocational and social picture the white youth were protesting against. Coalitions between the two groups tended to be short-lived, in spite of the rhetoric of white youth, with the exception of the most militant groups. It was the postaffluent white movement that captured the attention of the media and most outraged the adult world.

It was also the postaffluent base of the youth culture that allowed it to be transformed in a few years from a violent protest into a form of American consumerism. The commercial success of rock music was followed by the mass marketing of the clothing and recreational styles that had symbolized the youth culture. By the 1980s, for example, jeans, which once were a symbol of solidarity with the poor, have come to bear designers' labels and to be priced far beyond the means of the working class. Drugs, once promoted as sources of new visions, are now expensive recreational "equipment," supporting a lucrative, if illegal, business network. Youth styles reflect the expensive conformity of the "preppie." Yet many of the values and styles of postaffluent youth have now sifted down to less economically advantaged groups. Age has become a far more important factor of style and identification than social class.[7]

The change may be traced in part to the sociological generation between that of Vietnam and today's youth. The revolution of the protesters may not have had much permanent impact on the rest of the society, but it did change the environment of the youth who followed them. Schools, for example, became sufficiently identified with the youth culture so that their ability to train the young for places in a world despised by that culture became impaired. Schools became places in which to learn one's separateness and alienation from the adult world rather than how to cope with it. This became one of the sources of *anomie*, or "normlessness," for that next sociological generation, and their responses differed in several ways from those of the Vietnam generation.

While many of these young people also joined groups that could create worlds of their own separate from adult culture, they were much less likely to form the loosely tied agglomerations of the counterculture than to find tightly structured, authoritarian communities that would impose a firm order on the chaos they perceived around—and often within—their lives. Those who did not become involved in groups often lived in isolation, reacting with cynical self-centeredness, seeking to get what they could out of a situation in which they felt no responsibility for others or for the social whole. It is not hard for commercial interests to exploit such an attitude, and this has been one more factor in the common knowledge that youth compose one of the primary consumer markets.

But reentry into the economy as consumers has not been accompanied by reintegration into the rest of the society. There remains a sense of separateness between the culture of youth and that of the rest of the society; this is the legacy of today's young people, the whirlwind they have inherited. Parents fearfully watch their children enter junior high, as if sending them off to live in an alien society. The period of moratorium that Erikson attributed to youth is now more troubling to society at large because it involves a time to experiment not only with the adult roles to which one may choose to commit oneself but also with the option to refuse all such roles. Erikson discusses the need for the young to find an ideology—a simplified but compelling vision of the world and their place in it—to undergird the commitments on which they will base their identity.[8] Young people today are faced with a bewildering array of such ideologies, as well as a set of critiques of each that may lead them to refuse them all. Parental influence over that choice is often muted because most of the choices are encountered outside the usual sphere of home and family. Youth who somehow avoid this exposure or who are protected from it risk being marginal to their generation. Those who experience it may make commitments inconsistent with their earlier training, risking later psychological strains, as well as alienation from family or society.

Thus, today's youth culture seems to be fraught with both great danger and great potential for creativity. It promises a time in which values are created, defended, defeated, reshaped. It offers a world with limited adult guidance except from the economic sphere, which is concerned only with patterns of consumption, or from an educational institution, which is ever more turned in on itself.

Institutional ties are tenuous, and the stakes are nothing less than the shape of the future, both for individuals and for society itself.

FOR REFLECTION

1. What kinds of events shape the perceptions of the members of a generation? As you review the events that had such a large impact on the generations of the '40s and the '60s, can you begin to identify events in our time which are shaping the perceptual framework of the generation of the '80s? In what ways are these events likely to affect that perceptual framework?

2. What are the potential points of conflict among the persons of the three generations discussed? What are the points of creative cooperation? What positive directions can you identify for people of those generations involved in ministries with youth?

3. How can the Christian church be the shaper of the perceptual framework of youth in the '80s in any genuine sense? How can the church be the point of creative cooperation in the interaction among the people of these distinct generations?

2
Work and Entitlement in a Postindustrial Society

While most youth of the 1980s are not yet members of the permanent work force, the way they understand themselves and the things they hope for revolve around the world of work. Important shifts are happening in this area of our lives, shifts that affect today's youth, and we fail to realize that our youth are growing up without some of the assumptions about work and worth which have shaped earlier generations.

One of those assumptions is that any individual's primary social role is that which contains his or her occupation. The strength of that assumption may be seen in the power it has exercised in shaping such movements as those for civil rights or women's liberation. The person who is kept from full employment, or whose work is unrecognized because it is entirely within the private sphere, is understood to be a nonperson in the public sphere of human life. Gainful employment is the gateway to owning a public *persona;* its denial to any person or group is sensed as a loss of personhood by most adults in our society. Underlying that assumption is the idea that social recognition is given those who contribute to the public good. Riches have often been used as the measure of that contribution, with unearned wealth only respected if at least some of it is recognizably used for the public good. In addition, there has also been the religious understanding which sees work as vocation.

The process of modernization has changed much of that understanding. As work has been removed from the private sphere of life, a person's occupation is visible to those who share that private sphere only in the amount of money it provides and the life-style that it can underwrite. As the division of labor in the world of work has become more and more specialized and attached to large organizations, the particular contribution of any individual has become harder to define. And as a higher percentage of jobs has been taken up by management and service-related occupations, it has become harder to define the direct contributions to the public good that any particular person has provided.

Modernization has as one of its chief values that of measurability; we do not commonly recognize what we cannot measure. The current glut of material on methods of evaluation testifies to the difficulty of finding the "bottom line" for many activities. We are, then, less sure of the value of work.

On the other hand, the movement of the culture from one of subsistence to one of relative affluence has brought with it a new emphasis on the role of the consumer. The consumption of many of the products of our economic system is a matter of choice rather than of necessity. Yet for the economic structure to be maintained, products must be consumed. Private consumption, then, contributes to the public good. It is here that we have perfected the role of the housewife as consumer, and it is here that the current youth culture has found a place in the society.

Growing Up Urban: The Absence of Childhood Work

Children in earlier generations received experiential training that defined work and worth. On family farms, in family businesses, even in the sweatshops of early industries, children knew that their labor was necessary for family survival. Large families were welcome because the relatively unskilled labor necessary for economic survival could be done, at least in part, by the young. Much of this work could be done at home, under the direction of parents who offered training for and gradual access to full adult roles. Here, as a result of observation and direct teaching, the young learned not only skills but also attitudes and values appropriate to the work they did and the social position it reflected. Family identification was partly wrapped up in the nature of the family trade; good workmanship was a value taught and practiced in the home as a characteristic of one's identity.

Apprenticeship followed this pattern in earlier days. Often apprentices lived in the homes of their masters. They worked long enough and closely enough with such mentors to absorb the skills and the attitudes appropriate to the work. Occupational roles were a way of life. Young people were able to observe directly how interaction among adults at work occurred and what it meant to be an adult in the work setting. They learned this in ways now sealed off from most young people.

As modernization has accelerated, such holistic understandings of work have diminished, although we do depend on schools to offer some generalized work-related attitudes along with occupational skills. Learning promptness and regularity, learning to complete assigned tasks within given time limits, and learning to subordinate personal preferences and friendships to the task at hand have helped to prepare the modern student for the world of work. But any identification of the content of that work with their future roles is likely to be tenuous, at least until students reach higher levels of technical or vocational training. Similarly, they are more likely to learn about such occupations than to invest themselves in them, and as a result, the work or product is seldom identified with the person who is the worker.

In the home, even after the workplace had moved elsewhere, there once were significant chores to be performed by the young. Before the invention and widespread use of our current array of household appliances, many hands were needed to keep wood ready for the stove and ashes carried out; to do laundry, canning, baking, sewing, and other necessary household activities; and to tend to the family cow, horse, or chickens. This labor, though repetitious and less likely to have a visible product at the end of the day, was recognized as necessary and important.

Today, modern appliances and services, as well as the nature of modern houses, have reduced the household chores to a number of small tasks that can be performed in a short time. Even if the young are enlisted in these tasks, the tasks are minor and occupy little time. Often such tasks are recognized as tools for teaching work skills rather than as a necessary contribution to the family's welfare, and are dismissed as "Mickey Mouse" activities. Positive attitudes toward work are not successfully instilled when there is no personal investment in the work and no ownership of the task or its products.

This situation is aggravated by the fact that while parental norms may be internalized by the young as goals and preferences, it is the peer group that models day-to-day behavior for today's youth. In modern America that modeling is primarily one of the role of consumer rather than of worker. The economic powers have been pleased as the youth culture has become characterized by profitable patterns of consumption, particularly in the areas of clothing styles, recreational activities, musical products, food services, and among older youth, automobiles and their accessories. Identity in the youth culture is closely tied to style, and style is defined by these patterns of consumption. In this way the youth culture easily adopts the adult role in modern society, in which work exists to support consumption rather than as a value in itself.

In sum, youth today learn to seek and express their identity, not through the contributions they may make to the society through work, but through patterns of consumption. What they seek in future jobs is, then, colored by that expectation.

Careerism and the Decline of the Work Ethic

Characteristic of modern industrial society are the variety of occupations available and the related assumption that individuals have the right to choose among them. In fact, the modern worker is often a consumer of occupations, choosing work roles to meet personal needs and goals. The underlying attitude of tentativeness—the expectation that occupational choice is not a permanent commitment so much as a step onto the path of upward mobility, which may involve a number of job changes—contributes to this consumer view of the workplace. Each person follows a planned path through the world of work that is his or her own "career." Labor has generally been understood to be instrumental, but the goal toward which it is the instrument has shifted from the product of that labor to the enhancement of the life of the laborer in ways unrelated either to the product or to the work itself.

It takes a major change in values to support such a realignment of the meaning of work. The understanding of work supporting the development of the North American continent was the concept identified by German sociologist Max Weber as the "Protestant ethic," reinforced and reshaped by the American frontier experience. One of the contributions of the Protestant Reformation to Western culture, according to Weber, was the teaching that God can be glorified in the daily round of human work. In this view the process of building a culture and maintaining it, if that culture be righteous, is a God-inspired process. Early Calvinism took seriously the omnipotence of God, assuming that no human effort could change a person's status as one of those elected for salvation by God or as one of the doomed. But this election was expected to show through the style of life one adopted, including the contribution to the public good that was made by hard work. A person demonstrated elect status by working hard, by saving money and putting it to work by investing it in constructive projects, and by living a life of upright virtue. Work, then, was viewed as a measure of righteousness, and success was understood as the reward of a just God to the righteous.

The American frontier experience allowed this attitude to extend beyond religious interpretation to the practice and evaluation of righteous economic activity. In a developing economy private gain *did,* more often than not, reflect a contribution to the public good. There was intrinsic value in work, not because of its inherent pleasantness, but because the sacrifices it represented paid off. The worker had respectability and a sense of self-worth. The society gained needed products and services that contributed to a national feeling of worth. The value of work was primarily a *social* value, defining a family's place in the society and the respect it could command.

As the economy moved from one focused primarily on development to one involving a more mature form of industrialization, extractive and manufacturing occupations were replaced by clerical and managerial positions that (1) required more education, (2) were given higher status in the society, and (3) had a much less measurable, less visible product. The worth of work could now be measured primarily by more professional standards, by the level of expertise of the worker and the amount of that worker's time spent on a particular project. From the other end, the labor unions were also demanding that work be rewarded, not on the basis of productivity, but according to the amount of time given to it by the worker.

Thus, at all levels the meaning of work changed. Instead of being directed toward the product or deeply felt as an expression of vocation, it is now understood primarily in terms of time. A person's time is understood to be his or her own possession, to be traded to an employer for money at a rate consistent with the quality of that time, which in turn is measured by the level of expertise possessed by the worker. Thus, highly educated people, or those trained in valuable and scarce skills like plumbing, can demand a high price for their time, and those who have spent many years working for the same employer are granted bonuses and perquisites as payments for seniority—for putting in larger quantities of time.

Such developments fit the Marxian definition of alienation of the laborer from the products of his or her work. They also fit what Yankelovich, in his book *New Rules,* has called the "giving/getting compact," the expectation that we must give certain things in order to receive various social benefits.[1] Work becomes recast as a "giving up" activity. Pay, status, and perquisites, as well as a sense of respectability, are what we get in return. One of the additional changes he sees in our society is a denial of that "giving/getting compact" and a demand that life—including work—be self-fulfilling. Thus the goal of a career becomes not just the pursuit of more money but the discovery of self-fulfillment.

The career as a form of self-fulfillment represents a personal value rather than a social value. It is neither a response to the evaluation of others nor a contribution to society. If others respect one's work and if it is seen as a social contribution, so much the better, but these are not the primary reasons many modern people give for their career patterns, particularly young and well-educated people. Rather, the important sources of evaluation are personal and internal. They even have an implicit religious nature, since self-actualization is often treated as a higher spiritual state.

Today's youth are not likely to find this attitude among their parents, whose work values are those of an earlier generation, or among peer models who do not work, but they *are* likely to find this new view of work through what they learn in school.

Schools: Gateway to Career or Social Experiment?

Today's schools bear a heavy burden. They provide the generalized skills training that families are no longer equipped to provide. This implies at least two things: (1) students may be led to consider a number of occupational applications of their training; and (2) some way of choosing among them may be a part of the system. This is easy to observe in most schools, with the second factor institutionalized in the office of the guidance counselor, once attached only to high schools but now at lower levels also. There are two reasons to offer guidance to younger students. First, the schools reflect the growing specialization of the culture, so that students need help earlier to choose among elective subjects that will provide background for eventual career choices. Secondly, some counselors in the schools offer not only guidance to occupational choices but psychological assistance as well. Coping with life as a young person in today's society, and in the modern school, is a hard task for many youth, one for which agencies outside the school—including the family—are not well prepared. So the school counselor tries to help students with their problems or, if necessary, provide referral to psychiatric specialists who may be able to help students cope.

The primary focus of psychological counseling is on the individual and his or her personal needs. So the coexistence of career guidance and psychological counseling in the same office tends to place the choice of a career within the framework of meeting personal needs. This only reflects the wider culture of the schools, which pushes toward defining one's career in terms of personal needs and self-fulfillment in many ways.

Tests on which career-choice advice is based are designed to measure both abilities and attitudes. They are interpreted in a framework of finding personal fulfillment within the limits of native ability and educational opportunity. Students who score high on native ability and whose family backgrounds indicate freedom to choose among the best purveyors of further education are more often than not recognized as leaders in the peer groups, at least within the school. So the expectation of choice becomes the norm for youth, and the self-fulfillment theme dominant.

This trend has been intensified as teachers and counselors have been affected by recent trends in psychology. The so-called "humanistic psychologies" are heavily influenced by theories that assume a hierarchy of needs, culminating in self-actualization. In a society whose economy has made it possible for people to take for granted the meeting of physical and security needs, the self-actualizing goal is seen as possible, despite the lack of social support for realizing this goal. Regardless of its practicality, however, self-actualization has become the normative goal in much of the educational system and the expected goal of each individual's career.

Such expectations are not, of course, solely the product of the system of counseling in the schools. They have roots in the training of teachers, as well as in the general social milieu. They are particularly present in the consumer-oriented hours of television that provide much of the information about the world possessed by today's young people.

The expectation of self-actualization is not the only factor that has changed the perception of the primary goal of education. Perhaps even more important is the changing definition of work in the society at large, which is reflected in the schools. For example, most schools have retreated from actions that are now perceived as capitulations to the student protesters of the early 1970s. These actions did away with traditional grading systems, providing for "pass/fail" or, more popularly, "credit/no credit" standards in which failure was essentially not allowed. In many courses unsatisfactory performance was simply denied. But those changes, and the student demands that brought them about, reflected broader sources of dissatisfaction with grading systems. First, as schools became responsible for more than imparting factual knowledge, it became necessary to recognize other goals in the grading system, such as shaping attitudes and behavior patterns appropriate to the social system and the world of work.

On the other side, however, were three trends that worked against the movement to recognize such attitude and behavior shaping. These were (1) the crowded classrooms of the postwar population bulge, (2) the growing expectation that measurement of progress in school would be objective and specific, and (3) the growing civil rights and related movements, which scorned all measures except those of data acquisition as prejudical and biased in favor of the Anglo middle class. These combined to create and make standard a form of testing that was more able to evaluate the acquisition of specific data than the change in attitudes and behaviors. Schools and classrooms had to pull back from objectives that were not measurable or were potentially discriminatory.

The definition of work as putting in time rather than producing a product is also dominant in the schools. For some time most schools have had different tracks based on ability and performance in order to keep students of the same age in the same grade, regardless of their level of competence. Even with rebellions against such classifying of students, many schools have resorted to granting more than one type of diploma, so that both competence and time spent in school will be reflected. Only recently have we seen a movement to demand at least some testing of levels of competence before a high school diploma is granted, and in many quarters this is strongly resisted. Students who have given up a certain number of the years of their lives expect to be rewarded with diplomas, regardless of the quality of their performance. Their attitude is similar to workers on the assembly line who judge work in terms of time.

Teachers also define their work on a time basis and do so more openly as the schools become unionized. Bureaucratic systems have contributed to this attitude by setting up time–related standards for teacher performance. Systems of tenure and seniority reflect longer time–related measures. As adult models, teachers demonstrate the value that is implicit in the system, that time is the measure of work. Students therefore learn what is a growing feeling in the society at large, a sense of entitlement to social rewards. And this sense of entitlement is based, not on performance or products, but on the status of the workers as members of the society who have put in their time in the position they occupy in its structure.

The position they hold is also assumed to be one that provides direct access to other positions. That is, diplomas and degrees are seen as certificates of entitlement to careers with job descriptions that include a specific level of educational achievement. What one has learned in school may or may not be relevant to the work in that career; what is important is the possession of the necessary degree or diploma. This certifies that a person has sacrificed a sufficient number of years to schooling to be entitled to a particular reward for his or her time on the job.

The call for "mainstreaming" the handicapped, for racially and ethnically integrating the schools, and for opening formerly single-sex institutions to the opposite sex are, to some extent, responses to this understanding of schooling. While much has been said about the value of students' experience in a pluralistic environment, observation shows that for most students the experience of pluralism is quite limited. Performance tracking, career advice, and friendship groups most often reflect homogeneity and separateness. But while degrees and diplomas are supposed to be standardized certificates, schools are rated in the public mind. A degree or diploma from a good school is expected to provide more access to future careers than one from a school rated poor or mediocre. Access to good jobs, then, is through attendance at better schools, schools that are white rather than black, male rather than female, liberal arts rather than vocational, general rather than special.

The motivation is to *be* there, however, not to work. Attempts by teachers to demand a quality of work consistent with the school's reputation are defined by students as poorly disguised attempts to restrict the access to good careers to a traditional elite. Such attitudes may well be fostered by the climates of some elite institutions, where the "gentleman's *C*" is an adjunct to a career of working in the family business or managing the family wealth. But for those without such connections, many school-related aspirations end in bitter defeat as they discover too late that they have developed no marketable skills.

In the meantime, at all levels of education, and particularly in the public school system, teachers face classes of students poorly motivated to learn, whose various backgrounds cause them to respond differently to cues from the teacher or from one another. Many of the ways teachers have traditionally motivated students to learn have involved appeals to common values that are now questioned or resisted by at least some of the students and their families. So in many classrooms the primary agenda is a struggle to maintain order. Creative teachers often resign in despair or find themselves simply enduring the hours in the classroom for the sake of the paycheck, clear models of the new definition of work as "time spent."

As a result, we have seen a massive increase in the number of private schools, many of them religious in a somewhat narrow sense of the word. In such private schools the students tend to be quite homogenous in background and life-style, so that problems of maintaining order are lessened. A specific set of values is instilled and discipline maintained. Teaching is expected to reinforce consistently those values firmly set in the old Protestant ethic definition of work.

However, the value of these schools as certifiers for career entry is often questioned by private or bureaucratic groups that rate schools, both formally and informally. Training in such private schools may not prepare students well for working harmoniously in a bureaucratic system. The narrowness of the value systems may make it difficult for graduates of such schools to work in pluralistic environments. At best, their training prepares them for the diminishing sector of entrepreneurial work or for the lower rungs on the bureaucratic ladder, for which a disciplined and obedient work force is desired. The value systems of these schools do not protect their students from the modern version of the Protestant ethic that sees righteousness reflected in the consumer patterns of one's life-style rather than in styles of work. These narrow systems only limit the access to many of the sources of affluence.

Pluralism, Fragmentation, and the "New Class"

To pull together all these strands relating today's youth to the world of work, I will first reiterate that while our definitions of work have shifted, they are the normal definitions in the experience of youth today. Youth may learn to resist these definitions, but they will understand their actions as resistance, not as the norm. In this, they are a unique generation.

Their experience of the pluralism of modern society is also unique. Others may know how imperfectly we have integrated minority groups into the mainstream, but these young people have grown up with blacks and Hispanics reporting their evening news on television and with women lawyers, judges, doctors, and public officials evident in that news. They know that segregated schools are an evil the society has tried to address; few of them have had the experience of being in a totally segregated school. In TV shows, movies, musical groups, and the like, they take for granted what older persons may experience as obligatory tokenism—the mandatory minority person, the ethnic hero, the woman in a nontraditional role. If their families and neighborhoods do not reflect such pluralism, their schools do—unless their schools are a conscious rebellion against it. They can hardly escape the impression that there are challenges in the society to their particular way of life, their kind of person, their standard of living.

Some young people react to these challenges by welcoming them, seeing in them new ways to grow or broaden their experience. Others find the challenge intimidating, threatening to their identity. They seek out like-minded peers to cluster together and shut out the challenge. As they do so, they make even more visible to others the option they represent, affirming in their choice the plurality of options that actually exist. Pluralism, when it is as widespread as it is in America in the 1980s, begets pluralism, even in the reactions of people against it.

At the same time, a new kind of homogenization seems to be

taking place, one that is particularly evident in the schools and in the world of business and government. That is best seen in the "new class." The term "new class" is from Marxist sociology, from the attempt to understand the failure of communism to bring about a classless society. In nations that have organized themselves along Marxist lines, capitalists have been eliminated as holders of power but have been replaced by bureaucrats whose place in the hierarchy has all the marks of a social class.

In our own society, say such social theorists as Alvin Gouldner, the traditional power of owners and entrepreneurs, who compose the group ordinarily defined as capitalists, has diminished, while the power of managers and experts has increased. These people, claims Gouldner, are also capitalists, but their capital consists in expertise rather than goods.[2] Because of their access to information and systems, they have become the dominant class.

The educational system, as the chief provider of information and expertise, is the primary institutional base of the new class. "Professionalism" is the term which best describes the new class and the growth in graduate-level professional schools indicates its importance. Professional status ties back into modern definitions of work, since it confers on persons the right to put a high value on their time. It also defines a particular position in the various bureaucratic hierarchies by which modern societies are organized. To be a professional is to possess a particular level of a particular kind of expertise. It is to have the power to organize information or people at a particular level of decision making in an organization. In a modern, bureaucratized society, professional expertise is power, more power often than wealth or social status. In particular, since the new class includes teachers and others who process information in modern society, it can potentially control our meaning systems and our interpretations of the world. New-class values have become the norm in our society. All others assume the position of deviance or resistance.

What, then, are the values of the new class? They are those which their most vociferous opponents, the militant evangelicals, define as "secular humanism." They follow what in recent generations has been known as the liberal line. They are, for the most part, quite consistent with the stance and style of liberal Christianity, particularly as it is articulated at the denominational level. The new class accepts modernization. It believes in planning and other rational forms of organizing and mobilizing the society. It values social equality which is assumed to be based on equal access to education. It celebrates the ethic of self-fulfillment and seeks to provide a more fulfilling life for those who have not been helped to fulfillment by the current social order. The standards of that fulfillment come out of their own experience as mobile, educated professionals in an affluent society. The people of the new class care about people, are concerned that we have a safe and clean future, and define problems largely in psychological and social terms. They affirm pluralism, and decry rigid adherence to narrow values that they consider destructive to the full acceptance of other people.

Most church leaders would find little to criticize in such values. In fact, most, if not all, church leaders are members of the new class. We celebrate the movement toward a more humane society that has occurred as people with such values have moved into more influential positions in the society. We are pleased that these are the values most likely to be presented to our youth in this decade, and we will do our best to help reinforce them.

But we must be cautious about that. Already there are movements in opposition to such values, which young people will be dealing with as they grow up; and there are likely to be more, some of them well founded. The values that have served so well to criticize and ameliorate the abuses of power of previously dominant social classes are not always adequate when they become the dominant values. Reaction is beginning to build, and we need to examine its roots.

To some extent, the presidential elections of 1976 and 1980 were votes against the new class. Carter's campaign stressed the kind of rural personal virtue that the more systems-oriented urban new class tends to denigrate. Reagan's campaign was a revolt in the name of the older Protestant-ethic-oriented capitalism. The "Moral Majority" and other conservative religious groups express concern about the morality of the self-fulfillment ethic, and highly educated urban neoconservatives seek a return to their concept of a socially responsible elite to provide vision and leadership. Where there is that much smoke, there is likely to be some sort of fire.

What, then, are some of the weaknesses in the values and ethics of the new class? First of all, lowered productivity and low morale in much of the work force have caused some to rethink the notion that management expertise is a self-contained and transferable skill. The attitudes and values of the new class seem counterproductive in industry, as compared with those of managers who have come up through the production process. Indeed, new-class values tend to be anti-industry, in spite of the largely industrial economic base out of which the new class has arisen. In the long run, then, it may not be able to support itself.

More importantly, the educational base of the new class leads it to consider itself, like intellectuals of other periods, above the pull of vested interest. It is a fallacy, however, to think that any particular group can speak without bias concerning the public good. While their concern for others is admirable and their general desire to provide services and access to groups currently not part of the mainstream America is to be applauded, the position of new-class people in human services and planning creates for them a vested interest in the maintenance of a dependent lower class whom they can serve. Few, if any, recognize this or would approve of deliberate action to maintain such a situation. Rather, it appears that in their blindness or opposition to some routes to economic participation, they define as demeaning or exploitative some potentially productive forms of social organizing that do not fit their own patterns of planning. In their attempt to eliminate abuses in the business and industrial sectors, they frequently create lucrative jobs for new-class people as inspectors or overseers, draining out funds that could have been used to develop jobs for the underclasses. Programs for equal access may unwittingly rob minorities, the poor, and the handicapped of specialized skills training or job access because these programs are considered tools to keep them in inferior positions. The intent of new-class people to equalize labor often results in its opposite, because of their partial and biased definition of the nature of labor.

The youth of the 1980s live in a society that has recently experienced a genuine if unrecognized revolution, which has raised to leadership a new social class with a new pattern of values. Young persons are being taught these values in most of the schools of the society, through the media, and in most other contacts they have with the world of public institutions. In a minority of schools, churches, and voluntary associations, they are learning to oppose them. But in both cases they come to understand them as the reigning values of the society in ways that older generations do not often realize. At the same time, these values are too new, too untried over the long run, to be expected to continue without adjustment and change. Youth need both to understand these values and to recognize their unfinished quality. They need to be able to see clearly the weaknesses and misdirection of these values, for they will be called upon to use and redirect them when they become the adults of the society.

Adults who work with youth need to be particularly sensitive to what is going on in the construction of these values. There are chances here for youth and adults to work together to help create a better future. In our understanding of the nature of work and worth, we are in the midst of an exodus from old patterns to new ones. At such times, there is great need for the kind of faith that risks a springboard into the unknown. Adults whose religious faith allows them to trust in an unknown future may find, in youth, trusty companions on a journey toward hope.

Christians have an understanding of vocation that may need to be renewed and reshaped in a postindustrial world. The relation of our work values to the lives of young persons is particularly important because a sense of vocation is basic to our understanding of identity, and identity is a primary concern of those who are entering into adulthood. Adults will not be able to create new values out of their own experiences alone but will need to move into mutuality with youth, pooling the insights of their different generational experiences. The style of our work together may well, in itself, set up some of the contours of new understandings of work, of vocation, of commitment, and of personhood in modern society.

FOR REFLECTION

John, whose father is a hospital administrator, has just been asked by his guidance counselor to consider leaving the academic track of studies, at which he has had very limited success, and pursue a vocational track as he enters eleventh grade. What should he do

1. if his father, a member of the new class, disagrees?
2. if his friends are all in the academic track?
3. if he feels that he is entitled to a professional position or cannot be fulfilled in any other way?
4. if the particular vocational track at his school does provide a strong sense of meaningful vocation for someone he knows?

5. if the job marketplace is clearly more open to him at the end
    of the vocational track?
6. if all of the above are true?

Who can work with John in a mutual relationship to enable him
to make the right decision?

3

Seeking the Self in a Consumer Society

Erik Erikson, one of the more influential psychologists of the past several decades, has described youth, or adolescence, as the time when a person should achieve a sense of personal identity. This is accomplished, he says, when a young person adopts an ideology that provides a simplified, yet satisfactory, vision of the world and one's place in it, and when this vision and sense of place offer the personal security which enables a young person to break the bonds of dependency upon his or her parents.[1] Anthropologists have shown us how this is accomplished in less complex societies: youth are set aside for a brief period during which they may be expected to seek their own visions, which will guide them in their adult lives, or endure physical tests to prove their ability. During this time they are also taught tribal lore that is understood to be the exclusive possession of adults of their sex in their particular tribe. Then, during a rite of puberty, their entrance into adult status is celebrated by the whole community.

Many churches utilize a fragment of such patterns when they provide youth activities like church camps, communicants classes, and separate fellowship groups. These are often connected with services of confirmation or believers' baptism. But religious lore is only a portion of adult knowledge in the modern world, and there are few secrets about it reserved for this time of youthful initiation into adult roles. Our primary puberty rite as a society has become schooling, and the period of separation has grown from twelve to twenty years. At one time the work skills, knowledge, and attitudes taught in schools helped the young to relate to a work ethic as a source of identity. The ability to solidify that identity with appropriate behaviors guaranteed honorable jobs and respected places in the community. This whole process was reinforced and given value by the religious culture.

In the early days of the technological revolution of our century, it was assumed that this would continue to be the case, at least for the children of the middle classes. As Erikson wrote shortly after the middle of the century:

> Adolescence, therefore, is least "stormy" in that segment of youth which is gifted and well trained in the pursuit of expanding techno-logical trends, and thus able to identify with new roles of competency and invention and to accept a more implicit ideological outlook. Where this is not given, the adolescent mind becomes a more explicitly ideological one, by which we mean one searching for some inspiring unification of tradition or anticipated techniques, ideas, and ideals. And, indeed, it is the ideological potential of a society which speaks most clearly to the adolescent who is so eager to be affirmed by peers, to be confirmed by teachers, and to be inspired by worth-while "ways of life." On the other hand, should a young person feel that the environment tries to deprive him too radically of all the forms of expression which permit him to develop and integrate the next step, he may resist with the wild strength encountered in animals who are suddenly forced to defend their lives. For, indeed, in the social jungle of human existence there is no feeling of being alive without a sense of identity.[2]

Much of the student unrest in the 1960s and early 1970s may be interpreted as a rebellion of this sort, as students questioned the value of many available work roles and despaired of reaching them through the battlefields of Vietnam. In addition, the increase in the options of the workplace has made particular school teachings less relevant to the world of adult work, decreasing the level of com-mitment to any particular work role as a unifying source of identity.

Meanwhile, other ways of finding a solid ground of identity have also shrunk. Pluralism in school and society has called into question all particular world views. New values include keeping one's op-tions open for career development and accepting other people whose ideologies are very different from one's own. This often translates into a pattern of keeping ideological commitments open as well. How then, does all this affect today's youth? On what ground can they stand as they seek to become independent and find an identity of their own? For many, this is the question.

Expanding Choices/Shrinking Choosers?

We have carefully developed the concept of occupational options in modern American society and we have seen that the individual is expected to choose work and plan a career rather than repeat family patterns. But this is only the tip of the iceberg; the expectation of choice runs wide and deep in our culture.

The most evident example of the constant practice of choosing comes from our patterns of consumption. The wealth of styles, models, and brands advertised for people's choice is only exceeded by the number of products to which those designations are attached. Since most of our sources of information—newspaper, magazines, radio, television—are supported by advertising, it is almost impossible for anyone to avoid the barrage of choices offered in consumer goods without being cut off from most of the activities and ideas of our society. It is also difficult to avoid defining the self as a consumer.

Advertising in the media is, of course, not the only way we are involved in choosing among the products of our culture. We have a great range of choices concerning what we will read, listen to, or watch. We hear much today about the way our choices are being narrowed. Major networks take increasing shares of the time on local stations. Second or third metropolitan newspapers go out of business, and magazines die. Yet more and more areas are receiving the benefits of cable TV or direct satellite reception, which vastly increase the range of channel selection. The decline of general magazines has been accompanied by a growth of special interest journals, causing subscribers to exercise more, not less, choice. To find one's way through the confusion of competing sources of information is a formidable task. Yet each of these choices offers a slightly different view of the world. Additionally, the way one chooses to receive information will affect many other choices over time, including perhaps, those elements of a world view that might form an ideology.

Of course, formal education is one of the most consistent suppliers of information for young people. The growing number of options concerning what school to attend is multiplied by the further options of classes and programs within the schools. While some smaller private and religious schools offer only one program and a prescribed set of courses, larger private and most public schools offer more and more choices among their elective courses.

Electives first appeared at the college level, then at the high school level, and now have become an important part of junior high and some middle school programs. The choices made by the students will influence their future programs, their careers, and the ways in which they understand the world. Their choices will also define the group of people with whom they share a learning environment.

The young person's spare time is also filled with choices. Different forms of recreation, advertised through the media, become consumer "products" and demand decisions from youth. By choosing a particular kind of recreation, a youth will also be choosing a certain group of peers. If one chooses to take up skiing, he or she may have a very different set of companions than if he or she had chosen motorcycling, music, or football. Not only do the persons involved make a difference, but also a general cultural style is expressed in each recreational option. The highly competitive milieu of many sports is different from the cooperative environment required to perform in an orchestra. Subtle—or not so subtle—class differences divide motorcyclists from members of the debate team. And those whose financial or family situations prevent their participation in recreational activities with peers, because they must work or care for younger brothers and sisters, have their own unique experience.

Religion, too, is an option in today's society. America has always had a pluralistic religious culture, but most young people have been firmly enmeshed in the religion of their families. The religious values they have learned have been extensions of family values. The companions with whom they have been involved in church have been extensions of family friendship circles. This kind of uniformity has partially eroded. Both the option not be involved in any religious group and the increasing importance of the peer group have made it possible for even children of devout parents to attend the youth group of a church that is not the parents' choice or to attend no church group at all. New religious groups—in the form of Eastern religions, unique or cultic theologies, or conservative noninstitutional Christian fellowships—continually offer potential ideologies for consideration by youth.

Each of these options, secular or religious, offers a different way of organizing experience into patterns of meaning, and suggests a different meaning of the self. The values and patterns of life held up in each as the human ideal imply a different way of evaluating one's own worth as well as the path to greater worthiness or fulfillment.

These religious, recreational, and educational options place individuals in particular groups of persons who have made similar choices. They will be in the same places doing the same things. They will be able to converse with one another, quoting mutually accepted authorities, using the particular jargon attached to their activity or information sources. Following common human tendencies to make their world relatively coherent, the young will tend to make choices consistent with those of the peer group they find most available to them, perhaps eventually taking up the whole cultural package of that group. There may be no reason that a particular musical style, for example, should go with a particular recreational option, but because most of those gathered for the activity seem to like it, a person develops a taste for it. It is something which can be enjoyed with companions. If not, a person may withdraw from that particular activity to find another where people share similar tastes.

Involved in these choices also is the way one presents and understands one's own self. If a "macho" image is necessary to be part of a motorcycle group, members will stress those elements of their personalities most consistent with that image. The same persons may stress very different elements of their personalities in a Bible-study group. But as with the choice of companions, there is always a tendency to move toward consistency in the presentation of the self. A person will tend to make choices of groups and activities that elicit similar personality characteristics. And since the way we begin to know ourselves is largely through what we see reflected in the eyes of others, those presentations of self become our self-understandings.

At the same time, there is an underlying understanding of the malleability of human character. One is what one chooses to be. If this is assumed, it introduces a particular tension. If one can choose one's very self, who then is the chooser? If everything is optional, on what ground does one stand to take the options? For some young people, these questions are crucial, and the answers are unavailable. This, in the long run, is the ultimate in *anomie,* in "normlessness"; it is a dangerous state. Statistics show a remarkable increase in symptoms of stress, particularly among the young, in the past several decades. Perhaps the most devastating is the 171 percent rise in suicide rates of white adolescents between 1950 and 1975.[3] Our concern here, then, is not idle speculation, but a situation that we must take very seriously.

The Commercial Packaging of Values

The trend toward consistency in our lives has led people in modern society to reduce the number of their choices by creating "packages" of items or ideas that have become associated with one another. It is now expected that the choice of one item in a package will lead to the choice of the rest of that package, whether it is one that relates running shoes to natural food and folk music, or one that puts together rock music, marijuana, and long hair. Though these examples are contemporary, we can see, if we look, a fairly long history of such packaging. Perhaps the most relevant example is that of American religious denominationalism; each denomination has put together certain emphases within the Christian faith, certain styles of worship and of living, certain forms or organization, and presented them to potential converts as "Methodist," "Presbyterian," or "Baptist" Christianity. Evangelism has been a form of marketing particular packages.

Today the competition between providers of such packages has reached a high pitch, even though established denominations do not now emphasize their competitive relationships. However, says sociologist Robert Wuthnow, it is our very commercializing of such packages that has permitted the degree of pluralism we possess without serious conflict. So long as we recognize the rights of others to compete for the attention and loyalty of potential adherents, we protect our own right to do the same. Freedom of religion is at least in part the freedom to provide options among packages of world views and values. In a time when the primary image seems to be that of the consumer, religion becomes one more consumer product, sometimes advertised in terms of worship services conducted in air-conditioned comfort, star preachers, or musical extravaganzas. For many, religion is simply another recreational option.

Unfortunately, it is very difficult for an individual to form the kind of ideological commitment that can support and shape personal identity by choosing a religious or value package with the attitude of a consumer. As consumers we assume the right to replace products we have chosen if we tire of them or they seem not to work.

This is simply not a high enough level of commitment to provide a source of identity that can withstand change and difficulty.

Thus the mechanisms by which social conflict is reduced may create considerable personal and internal conflict or confusion, especially for the young. We react against the narrowness of those who would provide totalistic ideologies, particularly in an age which still remembers all too well the abuses of such ideologies by Hitler, Stalin, and their kind, and we are reluctant to present to the young any value package as if it were the only possible option. Yet when established groups do not offer *the way,* sectarian groups or the so-called cults often do. In the larger view of society they only add to its pluralism, but for those who join, they offer a unified environment that reduces options and surrounds the individual with peers who have chosen the same package. Often the group provides a sense of purpose which appeals to the idealistic, providing a strong sense of identity and self-worth.

But the cost of such a choice is high, higher than most young people are willing to pay. The maintenance of options may be one of our most universal values, and it prevents most young people from becoming committed to any group. In fact, the turnover rate in most new religious groups is extremely high, regardless of the common fear that cults permanently brainwash their adherents.

Rather, the value package that now seems to have the greatest appeal is one built on the assumption that each person has an innate and intact self—no matter how crusted over with social conventions and expectations it may be—which must be freed to reach its highest potential. This package may be wrapped in the language of humanistic psychology and the human potential movement. It may be packaged with the rhetoric of an individualized version of liberation theology. It may come through growth groups or consciousness-raising sponsored by the church or by some other voluntary association. It may be cast in the language of personal salvation.

Regardless of the package, the result is often a form of self-centeredness that is not given the negative connotation of selfishness. Rather, says Yankelovich, the duty to the self has taken on a strong moral quality.

"I Owe It to Myself"

The primary end of human life in this view is the discovery and

development of one's self. For the first part of that task a great deal
of introspection is required. Psychology has become dominant,
particularly in popularized forms. The primary sources of that "pop
psych" are those based on humanistic psychology—a logical choice,
since the humanistic psychologists have put together an understanding based on mentally healthy people rather than, as Freud, on the
mentally ailing who have come in for treatment. The theories of
such experts as Maslow are seminal. These assume a developmental
sequence leading to the full "actualizing" of the self. Some, including Maslow, have moved a step beyond, to some idea of
transcendence, but in "stage" theory this can only be achieved
through self-actualization.

While these psychologies offer a number of valuable insights,
they also include several pitfalls. Yankelovich points to one of them
when he writes:

> I have always felt uncomfortable with Maslow's notion of self-
> actualization as the pinnacle of a hierarchy of inner needs. Its appeal
> is falsely seductive, especially for students in elite colleges who thrill
> to the idea that because they are privileged students they exist on a
> higher level of being than those less privileged who, having to scram-
> ble for a living, miss the delights of self-actualization—though the
> fate of these unfortunates is not their fault, of course.[4]

He goes on to excuse Maslow from the blame for this misinter-
pretation of his theory, but we, too, are talking about the popularized versions of such work rather than its original form.

A more relevant pitfall is the assumption that the later steps on
the hierarchy of needs can only be reached by the mature. When
the young must be expected to live somewhere at the lower levels
and when we add this assumption to post-Freudian fears of high
frustration levels, we are afraid to present the young with visions
of the ideal person or way of life which are necessary to the development of identity. Thus we come full circle, establishing the
absolute value of the self in ways that are likely to erode its development.

The churches are often caught in this process. A general cultural
emphasis on personal needs and psychological methods has led to
a tendency to define the professional minister's principal role as
that of pastoral counselor. However, the psychological disciplines
out of which counseling has come stress acceptance of persons

where they are, denying the activities of the ideologue who would "lay a trip" on them.

The application of humanistic psychology and developmental theories to religion has resulted in a stage theory of faith development that has proved very helpful in tempering our expectations as well as in shaping educational curricula and programs. At the same time, the stage theory contains familiar weaknesses when applied without care. It is assumed, for example, that later stages can only be reached in the later years of a person's life. At best, we are told, youth are only capable of questioning the given tradition, not of transcending it in some form of universalizing faith. Since they are not expected to be able to think in the manner of higher levels, little is said about those stages. The unintended result is that we may teach the young to be critics without offering a better vision on which their criticism may be based. We give them the tools for breaking loose from tradition and parental guidance, but no center around which they may mobilize their hopes for their own future or that of the society. In this sense the theory of developmental stages becomes self-filling in that we do not provide youth with support in finding a focus for life.

As a result, many young people spend agonizing years in a desperate search for a grounded sense of self. Our implicit demand that their dimly perceived self be "actualized" becomes an impossible task. The best they can do is to accumulate experiences that satisfy some of their personal desires, hoping that this will be meeting lower-level needs so that they can eventually rise to the level of self-actualization. The working definition of the self becomes the sum of all those perceived needs and desires, since nothing else about it is clear.

What is not taught is the social nature of the self. If we understand who we are by seeing the reflection of ourselves in the eyes of others—and this is what most social and behavioral scientists accept as the primary source of self-awareness and self-evaluation—then introspection is a poor way to discover who we are. Even if we take up popularized versions of group therapy and seek the self in the company of other such seekers, it is hard to find a response in others who are equally self-absorbed. We eventually see that Jesus' statement that only those who lose their lives will find them is less prescriptive than descriptive. Only when we give up the search for the self is it likely to become successful.

The Search for Commitment

Daniel Yankelovich, however, notes several surveys that indicate a change in this pattern, a movement away from an ethic of self-fulfillment to one more oriented toward others. His firm has had a component in its yearly national surveys called "Search for Community," which has risen from a 32 percent positive response in 1973 to 47 percent in 1980.[5] The rise in percentage of young people marrying rather than continuing informal arrangements and the figures concerning an increased interest in religion also indicate such a trend. In fact, the move toward a religious expression that is more conservative may in itself be seen as part of this trend when we consider the stress on commitment in those churches.

Many of these trends indicate changes in attitude more than change in behavior. Future behavior changes are predicted, but hesitantly, even though the limitations of the individualistic ethic are becoming clear. The self may still be an important factor, but the shallow relationships and minimal commitments of a culture of self-pursuit have led not to self-actualization but to a sense of emptiness. People seek community because they are beginning to see it as the source of identity. Such a search for community may be seen as an attempt to reverse trends common in Western culture for many years.

The modernization process that has shaped our current cultural patterns has itself been shaped by processes modeled in the assembly line. Both work and knowledge require cooperative organization. No single individual or small group can possess the knowledge and skills to contain the whole. Therefore, our society has become a society of specialists, and each specialty has to some degree developed its own peculiar language and style. Communication between specialties is often limited to the areas where functions overlap. Our society can now be characterized by what Berger, Berger, and Kellner have called "componentiality," with each component separate from others, but joining to form broader patterns.[6] Humanly speaking, each component encourages its people to emphasize the specific aspects of their personalities and styles of life that will enhance the performance of tasks within the specialty.

Specialization of this kind often undermines the ability of persons from different segments of society to communicate clearly with one another. Their perceptions of one another may vary enough to confuse the sense of identity of each, built upon the feedback that each receives within his or her own groups. In order to reduce such confusion, people spend more and more of their time with those whose specialties are similar and whose behaviors are thus more predictable.

For youth this is a particularly important situation. If the tendency is to buy into packages that include life-styles and friends, we also need to consider the implications of such choices for self-understanding. A young person's understanding of his or her own gender identity is an important example. One of the directions of specialization in modern society has been a greater separation of male and female roles. As the workplace has been removed from the home, personality characteristics most valuable at work and those most welcome in the home have become progressively more distinguished from one another. And since, until recent times, the workplace was generally assumed to be the male province and the home the female province, the separation of male and female charactertistics has grown accordingly.

The role relationships of men and women have become more like those found in warlike primitive tribes—which demand warrior characteristics of the men—than like those assumed in our culture's agricultural past. On farms, for example, nurturing qualities are necessary in the men if they are to do a good job of raising crops and livestock. In addition, until recent mechanization led to enlargement of the farm's acreage, a farmer's work took place largely within sight of the rest of the family. He might be visibly strong and virile and successful in his business dealings, and still show characteristics now defined as primarily feminine. Women, on the other hand, frequently had to handle situations requiring physical strength, courage, and a kind of hardness we now tend to define as masculine. In urban industrial society there is less call for such overlap in male and female roles, and so we have compartmentalized them.

As a result, women whose temperament tends more toward instrumentality, efficiency, and strength, and men with more nurturant qualities, have difficulty in identifying with their own sex. The understanding of human nature which sees a central self to be uncovered and realized brings to such people the fear or suspicion that they may really be female selves imprisoned in male bodies or vice versa. Since the primary ethic is seen as the development of that self, transexuality and homosexuality become not only a behavioral option but a moral right. The modern self-fulfillment ethic often demands that sexuality be acted out, but what is at stake here is much less sexual behavior than the sense of one's basic identity. In this way, regardless of one's physical attributes, one's sexuality becomes an option, as so many other things are options. It is another part of a life-style composed of components which requires choosing a whole package.

Young people, seeking their own identities through commitment to appropriate groups and life-styles, find themselves faced with pressure to act out their sexual urges. While the innate self has such needs that must be fulfilled, the pressure is also strong because young people can best understand through experience the sexual nature of that self. Earlier psychologies stated the need for identification with peers of one's own sex in the preadolescent years. The popular psychology of today's culture may lead young people, particularly if the preadolescent period is prolonged, to assume that they are by nature homosexual and to identify with a gay life-style before they have matured enough socially to experiment with a heterosexual one. This is not to say that all homosexuals suffer from such misplaced identification, but current social forms encourage this kind of distortion.

Sexual identity is not the only choice demanded by our tendency to compartmentalize social roles, but it is one that is especially poignant in the adolescent years. At the same time, part of the componentiality of modern life refers to individual life patterns. Few people spend all their time within one of the specialized groups. Rather, our lives bounce from one to another. The person one is expected to be on the job is often very different from the one who must return home in the evening. Neither may be very similar to the person who engages in a favorite recreation, voluntary association, or church activities. We develop, then, component selves, often carefully separated from one another, each to be put forth in a specific place and time.[7] The passage of time also adds to this component quality of life; the separation of age groups in our society becomes so great that there may appear to be little continuity between what is understood to be one's self as a youth, as an adult, or as an elderly person. The self has indeed become an elusive entity.

One way to deal with this problem is to attempt to limit, or even eliminate, the components. One may simply refuse to leave the youth culture. This may be done by developing a specialty that is imbedded in it—such as rock music—or by serving its members through such professions as youth minister or teacher or by refusing to get a job and move out from home or by hanging around college campuses or settlements of street people. An older person may refuse to move out into the "golden age" group, trying to resolve a midlife crisis by ever-more-desperate attempts to look and act younger. A person may choose to live in a rural commune, where those who live together also work together, or may join a religious order or one of the new movements that provides a total community of work, faith, and daily life. For most, however, such options are neither available nor attractive.

Yet some sense of stability is necessary to a secure sense of the self, and some of the trends noted by Yankelovich indicate that people are beginning to take more seriously the idea that long-term commitments to persons, groups, and/or particular world views may provide the route to such stability. This may be seen now among some members of the 1960s protest generation who have regularized their relationships and who have begun to have children. And the members of the next-younger generation, rebelling against the anarchy of the previous generation, have in many cases settled into early marriages, reaffirming the nuclear family as the chief source of stability.

But divorce rates continue to soar, and recent evidence of increased domestic violence does not lead to great optimism about rushing into marriage as a solution to personal insecurity or confusion. Today's youth see this and they are concerned. The necessity of making long-term commitments is also frightening. Results of poor choices involving people are not easy to escape.

Social changes in recent years have taken from the young many patterns of expectation that previously guided youth into reasonable commitments. The ethic of self-fulfillment makes the search for commitment much more lonely if even committing oneself to a group arises out of the personal needs that will be satisfied by that commitment. Erikson has called youth a time of moratorium during which a young person may try on a number of social roles without the consequences of permanent commitment. The student movements of recent decades can be understood as an extension of that sense of moratorium into considerably older age groups. If the cultural trend is now toward growing up and making expected commitments, are we expecting from teenagers forms of commitment appropriate to the people in their twenties and thirties—those whom we have been allowing the freedom to experiment which was once reserved for teenagers? Can such a trend ever legitimately penetrate the youth culture?

Contemporary youth live under severe counter pressures. On the one hand, they are expected to engage in unlimited experimentation in order to discover not only a niche in life but also their basic identity. On the other, they are pushed to close off all options in order to commit themselves to some group or ideology that can guarantee a consistent sense of self and purpose. The tension between such demands is high, and those who learn to walk the tightrope between them are likely to be exceedingly adept and well-balanced. But the possibility of being pulled off in either direction is also high, and the consequences are liable to be destructive. The example of the sociological generations that preceded them is confusing. The input of older generations, including parents, is often distorted by views of our age as one of change so rapid that one can learn little from the past, or as one of a romanticized past that may be maladaptive.

Because the society is so compartmentalized and the period of training youth for public roles so prolonged, most of the activities of youth take place in the private sphere or in the isolation of the youth culture, far from the public places in which the broader boundaries of their lives are formed.

An image I find all too appropriate for the relation of youth to the larger society in the 1980s is that of a pearl in an oyster. Like the oyster dealing with an irritating grain of sand, our society has found its youth troubling. Like the oyster, we have encased that source of irritation in layer on layer of beautiful shiny stuff—all the accoutrements of our consumer society—until they are effectively walled off from the larger whole. The question, then, may be whether they can free themselves from so thick and tough—and seductively attractive—an encasement to be able to move beyond the youth culture into responsible active public involvment or whether we will try to keep and treasure that beautiful cultural artifact, ignoring the real lives hidden within it. Are there ways in which youth can escape into full public participation? If so, must it require the shattering of the culture in which they are encased? This is a question for the whole society and a particularly poignant one for the adults who seek the good both of the youth and of the society.

FOR REFLECTION

Brenda has moved to a new city because her father has received a job promotion. Her parents have purchased a house in a suburban area, and she has visited the public school. At her previous school Brenda had made "bad" choices of friends and had been in trouble with school authorities. Her father has offered to pay for a private school in this new location if she would like that. She sees this move as an opportunity for a new start, but she is also afraid that she might make bad choices again. How might the following factors have a bearing on her decision?

1. The discovery of compatible people in school, neighborhood, and church.
2. The level of her father's salary.
3. The strength of her determination to start again or the challenge of a specific new commitment.
4. The church and "package" of values she carries with her.
5. The components of her own self-image.

4
Youth and the Public Dimension

The combination of the alienation from work in modern society and the expectation that the home offers a haven in that alienated, impersonal world indicates that there are two spheres in human life, the public and the private. The educational institution, with values and goals separate from those of either private or public spheres, has emerged as a third sphere for youth, adding to the disparity in their lives. But for youth, the peer group and its school environment are the most important sources of meaning, identity, and activity. While many have been able to stay within those bounds by opting for higher education and careers in research and teaching, becoming role models in that environment, it is evident that the period of schooling is temporary for most young people. Current economic conditions make this reality more clear and immediate for many because the availability of scholarships, teaching posts, and research grants is diminishing.

Of the three spheres, the one that we label "public" is most alien to the youth of the 1980s. The world of full-time work or a career can be penetrated by few of them. Even less familiar is the political world, though it is the primary path toward social responsibility and public action. The history of the generation of student unrest leaves the current generation with the impression that students have an adversary relationship with established political forces but have little power to effect significant change. If that particularly large generation of youth in the '60s could not affect the political structure, there seems little reason to think that today's youth could.

The call to public responsibility is hard to hear through the welter of advertisements defining public participation in terms of consumption. The call to public responsibility is equally hard to hear from the safe areas beyond the barricades we have erected to protect families and schools from public disturbance. It may be that school integration has helped some students to personalize unrest—by getting to know individuals involved in such disturbance—so that even here they lose the sense of social structure that lies behind such problems.

Yet one of the reasons that many persons are so desperate in their search for a sense of identity is that in our culture we do not feel whole if there is no public dimension to the self. If our sense of who we are has no link with the history of human society as a whole, if what we do has no impact on others, we begin to feel that our lives have essentially no meaning. This becomes most poignant among the elderly as they face the end of life, and it is perhaps of next greatest import to youth as they look ahead to adult careers as a whole before plunging into the demanding day-to-day details of implementing those careers. It may be that the alarming increase in youth suicides is related to the sense of hopelessness modern young people feel when they fail to find ways to have any effect on the world or fail to discover any larger dimension than that of their own small private worlds, which are already beginning to cramp their spirit.

But it is not just individuals who lose meaning; there is also a corporate loss of purpose and value. We must step back and look at this when we begin to consider ways that youth, and their churches, must learn to speak to the issue. As we look at our society, with its division into public and private spheres, a diagram of the placement of major institutions would show church and family securely placed in the private sphere, education in a place almost entirely by itself, scarcely touching either the public or the private, and government and the economy in the public domain (see figure 1). Public values, then, are the values of those latter institutions.

In the case of economic values, the bottom line is—and in a capitalistic economy always will be—profit. It is a mistake to expect anything else unless we choose to seek major cultural change. We may hope to shape the definition of what is profitable by regulating or making too expensive those activities we consider socially de-

FIGURE 1

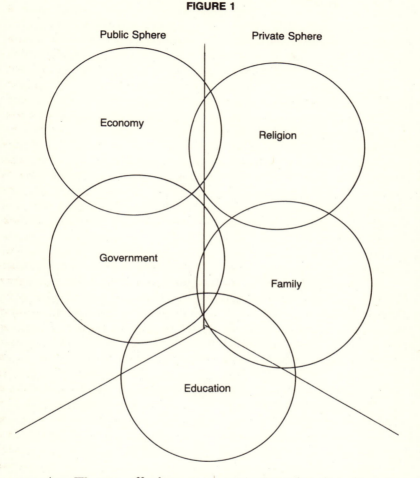

Public Sphere | Private Sphere

Economy

Religion

Government

Family

Education

structive. We may offer long-range projections that show how, in the long run, the more socially beneficial activities can be more profitable. But most of us, including the poor and the oppressed, are not served when an economy collapses. We must respect those functions that support our lives, even if we do not value the bloated life-styles of our present consumer economy.

The chief governmental values are those of order and justice. Again, no matter how lowly we esteem government at the local, state, or national levels, no one is served if we refuse its mandates

so that the public order is destroyed. The concept of justice, however, is something to explore more fully, for what we currently
call *justice* is an inadequate view. In modern society we have limited
the concept of justice to one of fairness. A just government, we
say, is one that treats all its people evenhandedly. This, however,
is only the first step toward true justice. And, in any case, true
justice cannot happen through the activities of government alone.
How can we distinguish fairness from justice?

For some people fairness implies that no one will be treated any
differently from anyone else. This doctrine is, in the traditional
phrase, "no respecter of persons." It is a least common denominator
of public life, only matched by that economic form of least common
denominator that says, in effect, that since making sales depends
on not offending anyone, only that which has no controversial
content should be manufactured, planned, aired, or published. Our
public domain has become the domain of the lowest common
denominator.

Justice, on the other hand, is the *highest* common factor of human
society. It speaks to those areas of hope and fulfillment that are
common to all human aspirations. It speaks not only to private
interest or personal development but also to a positive human
environment for ourselves, our children, and our children's children. It provides a hope shared by rich and poor, black and white,
male and female, religious and nonreligious, educated and ignorant.
It is humanity's highest common factor and is expressed best in
our religious tradition by the Hebrew word *shalom*. By its very
nature it is religious, though it transcends the specific doctrines and
patterns of any one religious denomination or congregation.

It is to such a common factor that the churches must address
themselves in their concern for the public. If they do not, the lives
of their people will become barren and the place of the church in
the private sphere will be threatened. Likewise, it is for this task
that the youth of the churches should be equipped.

Mass Society and Pluralism

We need to examine the channels through which people get
involved publicly in our total society and which have been restricted
from our vision for the past few decades. In the 1950s there was a
theory popular among political scientists that got lost in the more
radical movements of the 1960s. It seems to be coming back into

public attention and may help us take constructive action in the world of the 1980s. A comparison between what is called "mass society" and what is called "pluralistic society" characterizes this theory. In mass society, said the theorists, the direction of communication is almost totally from the top down or from a centralized organization of power outward toward a mass of fragmented, isolated individuals. In their isolation individuals have little power to respond to the power holders other than to acquiesce. At most they may withdraw, refuse to participate in programs, or otherwise exercise some amount of veto power. Their lives, however, are shaped by what they receive in the way of information and orders from the central power holders.

This is the model for such anti-utopias as described in George Orwell's *1984*, where Big Brother watches everyone. It is a model traditionally attached by Americans to communist governments and the centralized bureaucracies that have been developed to control the economic as well as political aspects of their societies. Yet, increasingly, our own society has become representative of this model. The creation of multinational corporations, the concentration of communications media into a few networks (themselves owned by such economic conglomerates), and the rise of the "imperial presidency" have been phenomena cited by social critics as warning flags telling us of the rise of a mass society.

Generally these issues are accompanied by warnings and have a negative image. What, then, is the positive image? Our ideal of democracy, particularly the kind of Jeffersonian republic of yeomen farmers, each with a direct stake in the society, seems fearfully out of date. Modernization requires centralization; it distances individuals from a direct experience of their stake in the society. Complexity requires specialization, and creating the flow of information is one form of specialization. How then can we expect anything but a mass society? Should we call anything so inevitable problematic, or should we learn to live with it? Can a mass society exhibit the characteristics of peace and justice, of *shalom?* In what ways?

The political theory we have been discussing posits an alternative to the mass-society model—what has been called *pluralism*. In this alternative model we assume a number of intermediate structures that mediate between the isolated individual and the centralized powers of mass society. Such intermediate structures represent general or specific public interests, but most people are expected to have membership in several. Thus, one person may have a personal investment in groups that on some specific issues are opposed to one another. Avoiding destructive conflict will be important in such cases. The pluralistic model does not necessarily assume bland consensus among groups, but rather envisions cross-cutting the pressures much as many boats do when they cut through one another's wakes on a lake. It is the overlapping memberships that prevent the formation of large and destructive waves.

The mediating structures provide human interaction at a small enough and local enough level to allow individuals to be involved as persons and to be affirmed in who they are. At the same time, such groups are windows to the wider public world. They have an interest in public affairs. Information about those affairs comes to the groups, where it is discussed, analyzed, and responded to by the members. As response is developed in the group, the individual finds his or her response affirmed, guided, and strengthened. At the same time, such groups carry more public weight than isolated individuals, and the response developed in the group is likely to find channels through which it can be heard in the public arena.[1]

This model is not new in this country. It is the sort of public pattern that intrigued Alexis de Tocqueville when he visited the country nearly a century and a half ago. He was amazed at the number of voluntary associations in which Americans were involved, and he saw that pattern as one way in which the nation had avoided falling into the chaos of "each against all," which he assumed to be a natural consequence of open democracy.[2]

The American model of the voluntary association has been expanded to provide the pattern for some institutions that are somewhat less than voluntary, but the important factor is found in their service as mediators between the public and the private domains. Most such mediating structures provide local groups that are small enough to encourage, if not demand, active involvement of all their members. In a comparative study of American and English towns of about the same size, Barker found that regardless of the size of their groups, Americans tended to have a far higher number of key positions in each organization. That is, the American pattern was to subdivide even small groups into subcommittees, working groups, and specialized offices, so that a very high percentage of the members at one time or another held responsible positions upon which the life of the group depended.[3]

In this way a sense of public importance is nourished in the individual. At one level it is a substitute for traditional European patterns of social class and village identification that provided a sense of place for immigrant persons who otherwise would have been left isolated in a new and comparatively chaotic nation. On the other hand, this pattern has called for a high level of involvement; passive acceptance of one's place in a given scheme of things is not enough. It has made a sense of public responsibility a cultural expectation, implicitly or explicitly felt by each person as a necessary dimension of the self.

We train persons early for these expectations, providing experience in the skills by which they can be carried out. Cub Scouts, Brownies, Bluebirds, and similar groups are treated as apprenticeships to their parent youth organizations. In rural areas the 4-H clubs offer group involvement for those aged nine to twenty-one. Lodges and secret societies, interest and hobby groups, clubs, chambers of commerce, service organizations, parent-teacher organizations, and "Golden Age" clubs follow us from childhood to senility with opportunities for involvement and service. This is particularly true in the broad middle classes of the society. The truly rich tend to remain in patterns of inherited status, as do the truly poor. In fact, one way in which it is assumed that the poor may rise from that inherited status is through involvement in such organizations. Expansion of these organizations into the lower classes is recommended as a public service.

Many of these groups also have national and international affiliates. Some of their projects and activities are related to those broader levels of organization, so that they pull at least some of the members into identification with and a sense of responsibility to a wider range of issues, persons, and places. In this way American society has traditionally called people into a comparatively active involvement with the world at large. Being aware and involved has made Americans more critical of the power holders of modern society than is true for citizens in some other cultures, who are taught to accept their places in the order of things.

Mediating Structures in Modern Society

This pattern of participation at the local level, however, has been strongest in forms of social organization not as fully modernized as our own. The suburban expansion after World War II threatened some of the processes by which it worked. As mobility became a significant part of the suburban life-style, it became easier for mobile people to identify with national and even with international organizations than with anything going on at the local level. Professional associations at a national level carried more weight for some people in shaping their careers than the opinions of local people or local organizations ever could. Corporate transfers from one region to another, particularly among managerial workers, who were the source of much of the voluntary public participation, became a common part of the career path. Political pressure groups interested in national issues were a result of the effects of national decision making felt at the local level. All of these factors contributed to the formation of a national sense of identity.and a more uniform understanding of issues. This situation was reinforced by the major media networks, so that national identity and organization were more relevant than local action. The local garden club, the local chamber of commerce, and the local political committee seemed to fade into purely social groups, powerless and shallow. National voluntary organizations fell into the hands of experts who could devote full time to establishing the place of the organization in the broader context.

However, these larger national groups do not provide all the functions of the earlier networks of more locally based organizations. The experts who devote full time to the operation of the organization become the only ones who can identify closely with what it is doing and becoming. Volunteer members retain little power, and when asked to make decisions, they depend almost exclusively upon staff reports. It is these specialists and not the grass-roots members who keep abreast of the relevant issues. Two consequences flow from this. Professional experts have a vested interest in maintaining their organization in its present form so that their positions will remain funded. They may then choose to lead the organization into less flexible or creative responses to issues and situations. More important, perhaps, is that the organizations which once linked the individual to the wider world through channels of personal involvement may themselves become models of impersonal, alienating mass society. This may be particularly unsettling to the young, who are at a stage of development in which patterns of identity are being forged. If patterns of involvement are not presented to them at that age, they may never seek them out.

The age category of "youth" in our society has begun to show the marks of a traditional social class and may be accepted as passively as members of traditional societies have accepted their positions. That is, young people may simply accept the designation of "youth" as their identity, without considering the consequences for the development of adult, public roles. There are consequences here also for the traditional American values of citizen involvement and freedom of choice. An additional problem is that no one can remain permanently in the youth category. Moving into adulthood from such passive acceptance of the youth role is likely to precipitate an identity crisis of huge proportions.

Traditional youth organizations with local, regional, and national ties seem to become training grounds for a small cadre of young people aiming for careers in managing various levels of such organizations among adults in later life. A frequent result is that a split develops between leaders and members which is more like the adversary relationship between modern labor and management than the positive pattern of general involvement and responsibility. Ordinary members begin to perceive the organization as the property, responsibility, and tool of the leadership. They participate minimally and only to receive particular benefits. They lose their sense of personal investment in the organization.

Are such patterns an adjunct to modernization? Are they, then, inevitable? Indeed, one may claim these patterns among youth as appropriate training for certain positions in modern society. However, uneasiness in industrial circles over low productivity among American workers, as compared with, for example, the Japanese, is causing a reassessment of some of our basic patterns of production. Most of the studies stress the need for worker involvement in the production process. This pattern is clearly in line with those traditional American patterns of widespread participation in decision making which we have been considering. Inefficiency and poor performance seem to accompany the loss of involvement in other areas of life as well.

However, American culture has never been one in which individuals develop a positive regard for themselves by identifying with social positions established by birthright. Americans traditionally assume that people are responsible for their own positions, or at least they believe that social forces preventing their mobility can be altered so that no one must passively accept his or her social fate. The pattern of voluntary participation has allowed a different way of perceiving and accepting a social role. In helping to form a grounded sense of the self, participation in voluntary groups and other mediating structures has led to an expansive personality type that, at its best, has been responsible for much that we celebrate in American culture. Such participation allows the individual to engage in the kind of interaction necessary to develop a satisfying identity. It also helps the person to understand that the identity has a public dimension, that one's opinion matters in this society, and that one's actions can have public consequences. No longer must all meaning for life be packed into one's own experiences and responses alone; it can be a shared project which extends beyond the self, beyond one's own space and time. A public sense of the self, then, becomes necessary to a sense of transcendence. Mediating structures in a pluralistic society provide one form of experience that can contribute to such a sense of transcendence.

Our problem today is to discover how that pattern can be reclaimed in a society defined as highly modern and postindustrial. Which mediating structures can nurture a sense of the responsible self? There are several, but it seems evident that one of them is— or could be—the church.

Churches and Church Groups as Mediating Structures

It may seem foolish to nominate the churches for such a function. They have been so thoroughly identified with the private sphere in the minds of most Americans that it seems impossible to conceive of them as mediating structures between that sphere and the larger public arena. For many people, the church has become totally irrelevant, something one grows out of—if, in fact, one was ever involved. In a secular modern age, why should we look to the church as a mediating institution?

There are at least four reasons for doing so. First, in a culture suffering from lack of meaning and in which means dominate ends, the church stands for values that are goal-oriented, that speak to ends. Many of the ends to which the churches speak are identified in the concept of *shalom,* of God's intentions for human good. They have a public dimension as well as one of personal wholeness.

Second, the church, as a religious institution, touches not only the intellect but the emotions and aspirations of people as well; it is more likely than many organizations to be able to mobilize the commitment necessary to change individual or corporate orientation toward the world. Third, the church is one of the few organizations left that has within its active membership three or more generations of people; therefore it has the potential to transcend the age segregation so destructive of the process of moving into a public consciousness. Fourth, the churches already possess regional, national, and international networks of involvement in the world, through which members can experience a wider sense of identification and action. Let us look at each of those points more thoroughly.

The process of modernization has been facilitated by our emphasis on methods of work and organization. As a result, one of the prime values of modern society is that of efficiency. At the same time, the growth of specialization has increased the diversity of the culture, and modern communications have put us in touch with people whose cultures differ widely from our own. Consequently, the language of values, of ultimate goals and ends, has not been part of the language of public discourse since it might introduce conflict. We can all agree on *ways* to get things done, it seems, so long as we ignore the questions about *why* they should be done. Such an arrangement is convenient, but in the long run destructive.

It is the "why" questions that give individuals a sense of meaning for their lives. Without a public dimension to those issues, people either feel meaningless or become selfish, trying to get what they can without regard for the needs or desires of others. They understand only the isolated individual to have meaning. No sense of pride or personal investment in the public dimension of our lives can endure in such a situation.

Religious institutions, historically, have a poor record on this issue, with each religious group claiming exclusive right to proclaim the true values and goals of humankind. The most vicious wars and forms of oppression have been carried out in the name of religion, broadly defined, for just this reason. How, then, can churches serve as mediating structures in a pluralistic society? Must they take the route of the "Moral Majority" and demand a consensus that would reestablish Calvin's Geneva? The American denomination model suggests not. Rather, we seem to have come to at least some level of realization that no single religious group has possession of the whole truth, but that all can raise questions of ultimate ends and values that need to be a part of human culture. Churches need faithfully to affirm their understanding of God's will for humankind while understanding their own limitations. This affirmation, when accompanied by enough humility to respect others' interpretations of that will, is the most pressing task of the churches in modern society. The word that must be heard is that there *are* ultimate ends for human life, that values are tied to the ultimate worth of our species, and that a primary task for us is to work out the appropriate expression of those values for our place and time. Each partial model can reflect in some way the overall vision of *shalom* that none of us can reach alone.

That word will never be heard in the way it must be heard if its presentation is only intellectual, only a presentation of facts. In the first place, all of our hard data concern the past. The present is not yet analyzed; the future can only be spoken of in terms of probability. Yet, goals and ends are located in the future. To speak of the future we must move beyond the scientific reporting of data, which has become the modern definition of truth, into areas of hope. This, of course, does not mean that we should ignore or deny the scientific data we have; rather, we should recognize the limitations of any one way of observing the world and our place in it. Religious practice in modern society includes much that is cognitive, as can be seen by the centrality given the Protestant sermon. It also touches noncognitive, affective levels in its music, its prayers, its architecture, its symbolism, and the fellowship of the community engaged in worship. Rightly done, worship can provide for people an experiential basis for their hope as well as a commitment to that hope, grounded in the science and knowledge of our modern world. Out of such a commitment religious people can confidently put into operation the values taught them in the church, values of justice or *shalom*.

The need for that kind of confidence and those values has never been greater. Many people, including young people, have given up hope for the future. Sometimes the things we say and do in the churches do not help very much. As we address social problems, we often paint dark pictures of the direction we are headed and never speak to the hope that is in us. An example comes from a recent book on new religious movements. Eileen Barker's sociological study compares members of Sun Myung Moon's Unification Church with a group who had listened to their lectures but not joined and another group who had had no contact with the "Moonies." She found few differences among the groups that would predict who might become a Moonie, but when she compared their responses to a question about what they thought the world would be like after the year 2000, only the Moonies had a vision of hope. The people in the two groups of nonmembers almost all gave apocalyptic visions of atomic destruction through war or accident, or of all humanity sitting on a garbage heap breathing polluted air, or of overpopulation, disease, hunger, and disaster. The Moonies, on the other hand, did not picture the political and economic empire we might have expected from them, but rather they pictured meadows with children playing in them and little houses with smoke curling from their chimneys.[4] Naive and impractical, we say, but only the Moonies had hope for their children. Only they could speak of a messianic kingdom where the wolf would dwell with the lamb and a little child would lead them (Isaiah 11:6).

It seems ironic that people must turn to self-proclaimed messiahs leading groups composed mostly of a single age category in order to find a word of hope. The theology of the Christian churches assumes that churches should be able to supply a responsible and faithful vision of the future of human society, one possible to bring about in God's good time. They should be better able to do so than new religious groups comprised only of young people—if only because of their intergenerational nature, which includes the elderly, who have lived out their years with faith commitments that they still find valuable, and the children, who are visible participants in the future hopes of the old. However, churches must strive to get intergenerational groups into lively, meaningful contact with one another in order to use that advantage. They have the facilities and the people to make this possible; they need to develop methods of constructive interaction.

As churches have the ability to provide meaning and commitment for individuals, they also have the structure through which those individuals can act out that meaning and commitment in the wider public arena. Denominational structures allow persons to identify closely with people from other regions and walks of life, even if the local congregations are relatively homogeneous. Social service programs and mission activities are channels to action in the world in the name of church-generated values. So, too, are political action coalitions, cooperative educational programs, and ecumenical activities currently available to provide channels of involvement.[5]

Churches, then, have the potential for mobilizing persons for meaningful public participation and the structure through which persons may participate. They also have the advantage of being established social institutions with a recognized function of serving the society. They might be among the most valuable of mediating structures, though their power to be such carries with it a danger of misguided attempts to dominate rather than to mediate.

The Formation of Public Christians

The place of youth in this consideration of the church as a voluntary mediating institution is of crucial importance. American culture has been developed on a model of voluntary participation that demands some level of personal commitment from its people. Ours has not been a police state, forcing particular behavior patterns on its people. Neither have we, as a people, had long-standing patterns of tradition into which persons are trained to fit without question or reflection. Rather, we have assumed that those things which benefit the individual will also benefit the society at large, and so we have made individual freedom a prime value in our society. At the same time, there has been a framework of teaching and practice, subtle and often unrecognized, which has equipped individuals with a definition of personal good which fits rather well into the genuine needs of the public. Private gain has been beneficial to the public at least partly because people have learned a publicly beneficial definition of "private gain." It is in this context that Yankelovich raises concerns about the developing ethic of self-fulfillment, while others raise concerns about the "me generation" or the "age of narcissism." On the other hand, the psychological needs tied up in identity formation have been well met when persons have recognized their genuine social contribution. In this way Americans have been able to be proud of themselves as productive citizens even while getting ahead personally.

In psychologies that address the identity needs of youth, we see the processes by which individuals assume adult identities in our culture. These processes reflect the ways in which churches function as mediating structures. The capacity of such structures to inspire commitment to ultimate values and ideals is particularly important for youth, who need to find freedom from the narrow bonds of family ideology and from childish concepts of the nature of the world and their own place in it.

A consistent danger in religious institutions is that, instead of serving as an instrument of growth, they may simply provide a focus of transference so that childish family loyalties become equally childish religious loyalties. The way in which religious institutions deal with youth becomes crucial at this point, for it is in this context that the transition into a more public consciousness generally will occur, if it is going to occur.

At the same time, that transition requires the background of an earlier sense of identification with the narrower worlds of family and tradition which we can no longer assume. High mobility, high rates of divorce, separation, and remarriage, and frequent changes of school and/or neighborhood leave the modern child with a bewildering array of options from which to choose reference groups, significant individuals, and other sources of identification. Even the child's religious training may reflect this. Family mobility may have taken the child to a number of church programs that have very different styles and emphases. If the individual child does not experience that kind of change, he or she may experience church programs developed in response to the basic pluralism of the society and its reflection within the church. Explicit religious traditions are not often stressed. Instead, the primary intent is to make children feel at home and loved in the church community. But they may be growing up not really feeling at home there, or even in their families, because they have a very vague and confused idea of the nature of the church and the family, which they have experienced only as fluid and undefined.

For youth programs to lead such young people into an attitude of questioning those tentative bases of identity is to introduce the possibility of utter chaos into their lives. It is young people in this condition who are the most likely recruits into authoritarian religious groups that offer a firm sense of identity and purpose, a resolution of the chaos into a meaningful form shared by a close-knit group of highly committed converts. For many, the ideology of such a group really does not matter as long as it provides structure for their lives.

At the same time, many church youth are quite ready to be

challenged and to move out into wider loyalties than those they have acquired in a fairly stable family and church life. Churches have traditionally met these needs through a youth program sufficiently separate from the rest of the congregation's life to enable youth to raise questions freely without disturbing those who would not understand their problems with church tradition and their search for a wider identity. Here youth can be separated from the children who are still learning the basics of the tradition and from those adults to whom their questions might appear to be a personal attack on the primary investments of a lifetime.

But what does the church do when persons in the category of "youth" represent not only those ready to question but also those who are not? How does the church mediate between an indistinct and shaky private world and a distant public one in its ministry to young people with such widely divergent needs? The answer to that question will vary according to the traditions and personnel of each congregation, the influences of its local context, and the social events impinging upon it at the time the question is asked. Some general comments, however, might help guide the thinking of church leaders as they consider this question.

First, the task of dealing with youth can never be left to the youth program alone. My research in this area has convinced me that most church children are lost to the congregation's programs by the time they reach the sixth grade. Up until that time they are generally under the control of parents who, if they themselves are church people, see to it that the children participate in religious education provided by the church, if nothing else. Since this is generally true, the children's friends are likely to be similarly involved, similarly willing to accept this as the natural order of things. But if by the time they reach sixth grade they still have not perceived other forms of involvement in the church, its church schools come to be seen as patterns of childish involvement that need to be outgrown. Baptism or confirmation become symbols of graduation from church involvement, occurring after the young person has already psychologically withdrawn into a world of a youth culture that does not include the church. Even though the junior high and senior high youth groups are advertised as something more adult and challenging, many young people nearing that age bracket have already dismissed church activities as "Mickey Mouse" and will not be persuaded. A church that is serious about its youth must find ways of expanding the relevance of religion beyond the church classrooms and formal worship before students leave elementary school. How this is done will vary from church to church, but an important factor is likely to be the behavior of adults in the congregation and their willingness to reach beyond the boundaries of Sunday participation to a wider and more challenging witness. Youth have no reason to define as adult behavior that which they have never seen adults doing, no matter how much they are taught about it.

A second point involves the utilization of the intergenerational strength of the church. Youth in churches need occasions to be by themselves, enjoying their own favorite forms of activity, dealing with problems and joys unique to their own age group. They also need to experience those problems and joys as part of the larger human drama and related to the experiences of other age groups. It can be both a happy and an unsettling experience for an adolescent to be admired as a model by a younger child with whom he or she is working. But whatever else it is, it is a growing experience, and one easy to provide in the context of a church congregation that can use the energies of its youth to assist in leading younger children in classes and activities. We wait too long to enlist the energies of our youth in such projects, assuming a lack of maturity that we help to perpetuate by not granting appropriate responsibilities. The church that is able, through congregational, denominational, or ecumenical resources, to provide that sort of experience for its youth in settings outside the local neighborhood—in work days or work camps or summer mission projects—adds another dimension to a growing positive self-image, one that may similarly be found in serving the elderly or the poor. A pattern of service, first within the congregation, then moving outside it, is one way to begin to involve youth in the public dimension.

Serving others, however, can provide a positive assessment of the self that may be an unrealistic one as well. Such experiences need to be balanced by those of working with others in a collegial atmosphere of give and take that allows for mutual correction and guidance. This is best done by incorporating the young into working groups that have a wide age range and that are focused on specific tasks in which each person's contribution can be seen and understood. A church that does not have active lay involvement in such tasks has little opportunity to model and provide these experiences for its youth. The youth program cannot stand alone.

Church youth can have the opportunity to reach out to other youth through denominational and ecumenical programs designed to expand their activities beyond the local congregation. Such activities allow the formation of a kind of public consciousness when participants join with strangers to affirm common values or to make plans for common tasks. If the activities of the local congregation have given the youth a firm sense of a place in the church and if they are taught that the real church is much broader than any local congregation, church young people are equipped for stepping out into this broader arena.

Dealing with strangers who are trusted because of common religious ties may be a step toward dealing with strangers in a more pluralistic setting. Experiences that affirm the trust given fellow Christians may serve as a basis for a generally trustful attitude toward others, which leads to a positive public involvement. Practice in public involvement through the local church can give direction to the application of religious values in the public sphere. Such public involvement can also contribute to the sense of responsibility that comes with working, sharing, and serving with adults, as representatives of a respected social institution.

Finally, then, the teachings of the church and the example set by adult members offer an ideological model to which the young can commit themselves. Worship services that touch individuals deeply and are expressed corporately have their greatest impact upon groups of believers who have worked together on common tasks. In a church whose life is vital, youth are likely not only to grow up into the full patterns of participation expected within their families but also to attract other youth whose families have not been involved and who are seeking sources of commitment. In this way, church participation among youth can model public participation.

New religious movements—the so-called "cults"—and independent evangelical organizations are providing high levels of ideological commitment and involvement in various programs for many young people who have found little challenge in the mainline churches. Perhaps the competition of those groups will awaken mainline churches to their weaknesses and motivate them to provide a greater challenge for youth. They will not meet the challenge of such groups by offering mild sociability. Rather, they need to note and affirm the notion that young people can make a difference in the world *now,* not just later. A church that demonstrates meaningful public involvement among its members, that serves as a mediating structure between private and public spheres, between individual and corporate interests, has many advantages over groups composed of a narrow age range or dedicated to a single public issue.

Without strong commitments, however, churches are not likely to inspire public action among their youth, nor attract them to anything beyond formal participation as consumers of their services. Such religious consumption can never be fully satisfying. People of all ages, ethnic ways, and religious traditions share a longing for the kind of peaceful and just society evoked by the term *shalom.* They want a secure and unfettered existence for their children and grandchildren. Youth, poised between childhood and the years of personal and public accountability, are most capable of envisioning such a society. They are also most easily crushed when it seems impossible. If they are grounded in a hopeful community, the energies they can put forth to work toward such a goal are tremendous. They need only to be led to that point where those energies are given meaningful connection with the wider world they are entering as they move into adulthood, a connection that allows them to become public persons. The church can become for them that hopeful community and that base for public involvement.

Youth ministries in the 1980s may be charged with leading the whole church into mediating ministries. These youth ministries may not be found on the fringes of the church but at the tension-filled center. It is a time of challenge and of hope. As those who have inherited the whirlwind find their way into public commitments, they are called to renew and rebuild the structures of a society shaken by massive change. There are many counsels of despair, but there are also glimpses of hope in current trends among young people. The time has come to move beyond the counsels of despair, join hands with the young, amd move out toward that vision of hope—with faith and with love.

FOR REFLECTION

1. Do you experience our society as a mass society or a pluralistic society? In which ways? Which kind of society is more in keeping

with our American tradition? Which kind of society offers a more hopeful or promising future?

2. Consider again the stories of John and Brenda from the discussion questions following chapters 2 and 3. Where are the mediating structures which might be of service to them as they make their decisions? In which specific ways might a church or youth ministry program serve as a mediating structure in their lives? Which elements of their decision-making process will contribute to their development as public persons?

5

Courageous Evangelism

Our concern in these chapters is how to reach youth. Many conversations among adults who care about youth eventually center upon reaching youth. Adolescence is a time of choosing and changing one's own authorities and heroes. Reaching youth can be a most frustrating objective.

There are at least three meanings of the term "reaching youth." A counselor is having difficulty with a rebellious girl. The counselor's concern is to reach or get through to the girl. A mother misses long conversations once held with her son. She complains to a friend that "I no longer know how to reach my son. We aren't on the same wavelength." In these illustrations, reaching youth is a communication concern. Often words have different meanings to youth than to adults. We hear an adult say, "I don't know how to speak their language." In America a distinct youth culture has developed which many adults do not understand. Reaching youth presents a difficult communication challenge.

The second meaning of the term refers to reaching youth with the gospel. We usually consider those youth who are "reached" to be those who "have salvation." Those youth who are "unreached" are those who do not recognize the love of Christ.

Yet the term also has a third meaning when it describes adolescents who are at a "reaching stage" of life. It speaks of youth who are reaching for life's meaning, reaching with doubts and questions, reaching for their place in the world.

In the first meaning, reaching youth is a concern of communication. In the second, it is a concern of evangelism; and in the third it is a concern of faith development. The three meanings are inherent in our approach as we explore the meaning of evangelism, the whole gospel, conversion, nurture, and the culture of today's adolescent. Our concern is to reach youth, trying to understand who they are and how the message of Christ can be *their* good news!

Adolescents are people. They are like you and me. They breathe just as we breathe; they hope just as we hope; they need the gospel just as we need the gospel. Some adolescents are more articulate about their faith than many adults. Like some adults, some youth are immature in their faith. Adolescents are not "little adults" any more than adults are "ancient adolescents." But youth are people who are at a unique stage of human life. Adolescents receive an inherited faith in which they grow and mature. They are also challenged by the task of shaping and claiming their own faith. Because they are at this unique place in their lives, adolescents require a particular approach from those who would engage them with the gospel. Such an approach may be called "courageous evangelism" because it requires risk by the person who would help youth shape their faith.

The Evangelistic Question of Youth Ministry

What is the evangelistic question of youth ministry? It may be asked in two ways: "How can we engage youth with the fullness of the gospel?" or "How can youth recognize with us the fullness of Christ?"

Those are the evangelistic questions, but what we frequently assume to be evangelistic questions are really *marketing* questions. Marketing and evangelism are related, but they are not identical; we cheapen evangelism when we use the two concepts interchangeably.

The marketing questions are: "How can we reach the most youth with the gospel?" or "How can the most youth be saved?" These are like other marketing questions, such as, "How can we reach the most youth with our brand of toothpaste?"

Evangelism is concerned with more than merely purchasing or accepting a product. The central concern of evangelism is not just how many persons claim to be Christians, but what is the level of their relationship with Jesus Christ? What we want for young people, as well as for adults, is not a superficial attachment to Jesus

Christ, but an experience of the fullness of discipleship at each individual's particular point in life.

The problem pivots around the modern preoccupation of the church with the "saved-lost" dichotomy. Jesus attempted to counteract such a limited perspective. Jesus was not just concerned that people have faith in God but that faith make a transforming difference in their lives. Consider his parable about the sheep and the goats. At judgment day God will divide people into one group or the other. But what is the criterion by which the division is made? Servanthood will be the criterion. Did we feed the hungry, visit the imprisoned, and so forth? (Matthew 25:31-46). Again Jesus said, "Not everyone who calls me, 'Lord, Lord' will enter the kingdom of Heaven, but only those who do the will of my heavenly Father" (Matthew 7:21, NEB).

The gospel is compromised by the spiritual elitism which is implicit in statements like "I'm saved; you're lost. I'm right; you're wrong. I've found it; you haven't." Such self-pronouncements and judgments leave little room for God, and they lack the humility of which Jesus so often spoke. Salvation is God's business. Who has salvation and who does not? Who is righteous and who is not? These are questions only God can answer. The words of salvation are gracious when God pronounces them, but the same words sound elitist as self-pronouncements.

Salvation is not something you can wear like an achievement. Rather than pronounce yourself saved, it is a much more appealing witness to pronounce yourself loved, or to pronounce yourself graced, or to pronounce yourself forgiven. Being loved and graced and forgiven by God are true and available for everyone. Salvation, on the other hand requires God's action and our response. Thomas Troeger says, "The mark of the saved is that they leave judgment in God's hands while they serve the world with their own."[1]

Let us pose the question in another way: When we think of evangelizing youth, what group of youth do we have in mind? Don't we immediately think about the unreached or the unsaved? We assume there is no evangelistic task with young people who are already Christians except to convince them to convince other young people to make the same decision. We need to rethink those assumptions.

I need to be evangelized, and I've made hundreds of decisions to follow Jesus Christ. There are at least two reasons why I need to be evangelized. The first is that most of my decisions for faith in Christ don't last. They are temporary, short-lived, halfhearted. I'm sincere at the moment, but I don't stay with it. My second reason for needing to be evangelized is that I have never been able to give my whole existence to Jesus Christ in one decision. While I *think* I am doing this, I never really do it. There are always unredeemed parts of my life. I'm like Paul; even though he was a vehement follower of Christ, still he confessed, "I cannot understand my own behavior. I fail to carry out the things I want to do, and I find myself doing the very things I hate" (Romans 7:15, *The Jerusalem Bible*).

I am not fully evangelized until I can share in Paul's claim that "it is no longer I who live, but it is Christ who lives in me" (Galatians 2:20, TEV).

I believe young people are in this same situation. The evangelistic task with youth is much broader than we have conceived it to be. All young people need to be evangelized until Christ permeates their beings.

Is evangelism only for the unreached? We must return to that "saved–lost" dichotomy. The problem is that we have too often believed that evangelism is a task undertaken by the reached or saved in behalf of the unreached or lost.

But there is another category of people, in part unredeemed, in part redeemed, who are the "reaching" people. "We shall become mature people, *reaching* to the very height of Christ's full stature" (Ephesians 4:13, TEV, author's emphasis).

For most of my life, I've been a part of the reaching group, reaching for Christ in my life, reaching to be evangelized. And evangelism is for both the *unreached* and the *reaching*. On this side of the grave, we must agree with Paul that we never fully arrive. "It is not to be thought that I have already achieved all this. I have not yet reached perfection, but I press on, hoping to take hold of that for which Christ once took hold of me" (Philippians 3:12, NEB). So evangelism is for the *reaching* as well as the u*nreached*. It isn't that speaking of the saved and lost is wrong. To do so just isn't precise.

I do not mean to encourage a lack of concern for unreached youth. Quite the contrary. I often pray for the young people in my own church who have yet to make their first decision in Christ as Lord and Savior. That is rightfully a concern of the faithful. But a concern for the unreached deteriorates into merely a matter of marketing if you consider faith to be something you can possess by a single decision or action of your life: either you have made *the* faith decision, or you have not. This perspective tends to communicate that you can purchase faith just as you purchase a car. But one of the differences between buying a Chevrolet and receiving salvation is that your Chevrolet will never look as good nor be worth as much as on the day you bought it, while your salvation has the opportunity to appreciate in value. Your faith should never again be as thin as it was on the day of your baptism—when it had yet to be tested by doubt, yet to be broadened by experience, yet to be nurtured by friendships, yet to be challenged by the Spirit. The *crucial* issue of evangelism is not only the number of people who have faith in Christ but the depth of the journey of those who do.

A *onetime* faith decision is only important to me until it is made. From that time on, like an automobile that has just been purchased, it depreciates in value. There is something compelling to others about a *first-time* decision for Christ. No person who ministers with youth can deny the thrill of seeing a young person with whom one has a relationship make a sincere, converting decision. The newness of the youth's salvation very often breathes freshness into that of the adult. But the first decision for Christ must not be the only thing that attracts us to the Christian experience. There is also something very compelling about the lives of persons who have been graced by God over the years. We must be challenged by the newness of faith in those who are launching the faith journey while we are also inspired by the depth of faith in those who have encountered truth on the frontiers.

The task of evangelism is never just to bring persons to Jesus and leave them there. That is never enough. The task is to issue an invitation to them to walk with you toward Christ.

Evangelism Without Delay

Some adults are tempted to minimize the importance of evangelism with youth. They cite the immense pressures and challenges that our culture already places on youth. Some of life's most important decisions are faced in the teen years. Why increase the burden on youth? Yet it is precisely because youth are at a reaching stage that faith provides an integral resource for adolescents responding to the pressures, challenges, and decisions of the teen years. The typical teenager reaches for faith to answer the questions: Upon what foundation will I build my life? What is ultimately trustworthy? Where is my place in the world? Faith is the most trustworthy foundation upon which an adolescent can stand as he or she faces an amazing array of choices and alternatives.

Adolescence is like being given a ready-made and furnished house. After you live in the house and acquire new resources, you become dissatisfied with the house that someone else has decorated and designed. Most adolescents reach in an upward and outward direction as they discover that the walls, foundation, and roof of their childhood "house" are pliable and can be reshaped into something more pleasing and personal. Some youth mercilessly tear down the old structure. Some youth subtly remodel their lives. Few youth will examine deeply what has already been built into the house. Adolescence is a time of seeking after what is new, not what is past. Young adults are more likely to look back upon their past and integrate it into their faith, while adolescents are reaching for a newfound faith.

If faith in Jesus Christ is the most trustworthy foundation upon which this reaching for new faith can occur, then we must be courageous evangelists without delay.

Courageous Evangelism—How Does It Work?

James Fowler says:

> I believe faith is a human universal. We are endowed at birth with nascent capacities for faith. How these capacities are activated and grow depends to a large extent on how we are welcomed into the world and what kinds of environments we grow in. Faith is interactive and social; it requires community, language, ritual and nurture. Faith is also shaped by initiatives from beyond us and other people, initiatives of spirit or grace.
>
> Faith is an orientation of the total person, giving purpose and goal to one's hopes and strivings, thoughts and actions.[2]

Faith is fundamental to life, and adolescents are at the very beginning of rooting their lives and giving them meaning. I am convinced that for youth, faith is a fundamental trust that gives their often confused worlds what little confidence they experience. They ask the faith question in terms of trust:

1. In what can I ultimately trust? What is ultimately dependable?

2. Can I trust myself? How much can I count on myself without being disappointed?
3. Can I trust others? How much can I count on others without being disappointed?
4. Can I trust God? How much can I count on God without being disappointed?

All of these are foundational questions of faith. James Fowler describes faith as a meaning-making activity, and that it is. For youth, the faith questions are first of all questions of trust. Trust is the basis upon which youth carve out their own identities.

Adolescence is one of the most change-oriented times in life. Because it is characterized by so many rapid changes, R. S. Lee likens it to infancy:

> Adolescence, the second infancy, prepares him to take his place in that world and make his life there as a separate and relatively independent individual. For that he has to undergo deep-seated emotional adjustments, by which he acquires a new outlook, accepts new responsibilities, and takes his place as an equal among men, putting the subordinate role of childhood behind him.[3]

Compared to the toughness, resiliency, and stability that they usually show during childhood years, teenagers often appear to be taking one step forward and three steps backward. They live with more self-doubt, more rebellion, more instability than during their childhood years. Their bodies are changing. Sexuality, and their new awareness of it, makes them often awkward, clumsy, flighty, infatuated, and preoccupied with self. If one of the prime tasks of adolescence is reaching for personal faith and if faith is life's foundation, then we can assume that adolescence is a time to establish new priorities for everything. A sensitive, courageous evangelist can be a precious resource to the young person in this process.

Youth are often urged to buy into Christianity simplistically or superficially. They are therefore led to the erroneous belief that they have dealt with faith in their baptism or confirmation as a once-and-for-all decision. They are surprised to learn that there are many more decisions of faith to be made, including some that might very well be painful and costly. These youth become disillusioned and feel betrayed by adults who never prepared them for such a reality.

What I am describing makes a great deal of difference in the content of our evangelistic message to youth. Either of these messages can be communicated to youth:

1. "Let us discover Christ together. Walk with me as we discover through each other the fullness of what Christ means."
2. "You need Jesus Christ in your life. You need to be saved and baptized. I am concerned for your 'lostness.'"

One message exhibits mutuality. The other is vulnerable to elitism.

Our problem as adults who care about youth is the inclination, because of our head start, to leave youth behind us, to walk on ahead, and not to be vulnerable enough to walk alongside them. We feel that youth will become disillusioned if they discover their adult sponsors have doubts and struggles and questions, as well as joys. What if they find out that there are unredeemed parts of our lives? What if they find out exactly what those parts are and point them out to us? *We are frightened of mutuality with youth.* We are likely to fear trusting youth enough to reveal ourselves as we really are, behind our masks.

The adult who wants to be truly evangelistic with youth will be a confessional adult. Such an adult will trust youth to the extent that he or she will walk alongside youth, sharing the hurts, joys, victories, and defeats. Young people are mature enough to handle mutuality. Indeed, as we open our lives to them, they are prodded to open their lives to us, and our relatedness to Christ becomes a deeper reality. But that takes courage. Courageous evangelism is not exemplified by the preacher who stands before ten thousand teenagers and invites their decision. Courageous evangelism is demonstrated by the adult who will sit beside one teenager and share the ongoing story of his or her own faith pilgrimage—complete with valleys and mountaintops. Youth need courageous evangelists.

When that occurs, you become, as Paul said to the Philippians, one of those who "must work out your own salvation in fear and trembling" (Philippians 2:13, NEB).

Youth are not fragile, nor are they retarded adults. They, for the most part, become as dissatisfied with easy answers as we do. They can ask sophisticated questions requiring provocative answers. We must beware of sharing a shallow faith that breaks down before we get home from church.

The gospel does not deserve the simplistic ways it is often communicated to youth. We sometimes do this in the name of being sensitive to the "unsophisticated" level of youth who need a simple gospel. Indeed, the Christian message *is* simple, if we mean that it is foundational or fundamental. But the message is not simplistic; it cannot be reduced to formulas, slogans, or clichés which are intellectually lacking and emotionally exploitative. From what we know of the developmental needs of youth, we can conclude that to present youth with a simplistic faith is to be insensitive to them.

As adults involved in ministry with youth, we must focus upon the fundamentals or basics of faith with teenagers. The fundamentals of faith will not allow us to make faith simplistic nor to trivialize it. The gospel is more than loving others or being moral people or hoping for world peace. Some redemptive word must be at the heart of our message, which makes it good news. That living word is Jesus Christ. John Westerhoff has said, "Only someone for whom the life, death, and resurrection of Jesus Christ is ultimately decisive may be called a Christian."[4] Fundamentally, faith is a basic trust that enables adolescents to reach beyond themselves. The courageous evangelist is the one who, in reaching beyond himself or herself, can model trust for youth.

Holistic Evangelism and Youth

Let us return to the question "What is evangelism?" The root of the word means proclaiming good news. And what is the good news? The good news of Jesus that was on his lips and in his teachings more than any other is of the coming kingdom of God. When we offer the good news to youth, there are two realities which we must have the courage to help them consider.

The first reality is that Christ intends to be the Lord of our lives. When we speak of God's coming reign, the reign of the kingdom of God in our lives, we are speaking of Christ's ever-deepening personal reality. Through the process of discipleship we become the persons God intends us to be.

The second reality is that Christ intends to be the Lord of the world. When we speak of Christ's coming reign, the reign of the kingdom of God in the world, we are speaking of Christ's ever-deepening reality throughout the universe. In the process of reconciliation the world becomes what God has in mind for it to be.

Evangelism is an invitation to the kingdom. It requires a personal as well as a social witness. Without both, we promote a half-gospel, not a whole one. We seek for youth, as well as for ourselves, a whole gospel at whatever level they, and we, can encounter it. In chapter 7 we will explore the meaning of a cultural witness to Christ with adolescents. It is enough now to say that a courageous evangelism with youth will seek both a cultural and personal witness to Jesus Christ.

Youth are reaching for a trustworthy foundation upon which to build the structure of their lives. The whole gospel of Jesus Christ is the most trustworthy and compelling good news we have to share!

FOR REFLECTION

1. Youth today live with many kinds of particular frustrations and difficulties. Listen to these voices:

- "My dad and I can't talk. I think I'm afraid of him. Maybe that's why I hang out over here at the park every night."
- "I want to trust him; he's the first person I've ever felt like I could trust. But now he wants me to run away with him and I can't make up my mind. Please help me."
- "All week long nobody talks to me except in giggles. So when the Friday party comes, I get so drunk and act so crazy that it doesn't matter anymore—at least for a while."
- "Nothing I ever do is right. I couldn't take it anymore. When I saw the razor blade, it just seemed like the easy way out."
- "I'm sorry; sometimes I just sit down and cry. I need someone to pass the tissues then."
- "I just have all this energy; I want to reach out to people and help them, but they seem to be afraid of me."

How might a courageous evangelist respond to these persons?

2. Have you ever engaged in courageous evangelism? Describe the circumstances. How did you feel about this approach? Were you able to trust the young people with whom you were engaged with your own faith story?

6

Conversion Without End

Conversion is the result of effective evangelism. Conversion is a changeover, a radical reorientation, a transformation from one thing to something else. Personal conversion is the transformation from the "old me" to the "new me." Christian conversion is the change from self-consciousness to Christ-consciousness.

The Paradox of Conversion for Youth

"Self-conscious" is a particularly appropriate term for adolescents. It is a term very typical of their unique life situation. Self-consciousness is a developmental characteristic which youth must overcome if they are to move toward a deeper maturity as adults. To do so is no small challenge. The term "self-consciousness" has two meanings that are applicable to the experience of youth.

First, to be self-conscious is to be awkward, unsure, uneasy with oneself. It is to be too much concerned about appearance and impression. A young person might say, "I was very self-conscious at the party surrounded by all those strangers." A person who is self-conscious in this sense is embarrassed about "who I am" or "how I appear" and is easily intimidated because of the lack of a strong sense of identity.

Second, to be self-conscious can mean to be egocentric, preoccupied with one's own self. This is not necessarily to be conceited, but rather to be very much occupied with one's personal agenda. Youth are legitimately busy with themselves, for there is much in their lives to explore and sort out. This preoccupation is something they must eventually overcome by finding a larger perspective. Indeed, a mature Christian is one who empties himself or herself by putting Christ and others first (see Philippians 2:6–7, RSV). But for youth, totally enmeshed in adolescent struggles, overcoming this preoccupation with self is nearly an impossible task.

If we consider these two meanings of self-consciousness together, we understand something of the paradox which teenagers face. On the one hand is a basic insecurity about their self-worth; on the other is a preoccupation with themselves. Conversion for youth implies, in this developmental perspective, the eventual transformation from insecurity to self-affirmation. It implies, as well, a transformation from preoccupation with themselves to an appropriate placement of their selves into a larger context of meaning and trust.

In this context an encounter with Christ is clearly good news for youth, for it affirms them as gifted, God-created persons with inherent value and purpose. An encounter with Christ also helps youth to find themselves in relation to God and to other people. It enables them to get their priorities straight, and it provides a context for ultimate meaning and trust. *Young people can, then, overcome the developmental paradox of self-consciousness through an encounter with Christ.*

The Christian transformation moves us from self-consciousness to Christ-consciousness but does not imply that our selves are no longer important. Rather, Christ-consciousness implies that we think of ourselves as Christ thinks of us. We are called to discover who we really are—the whole person who was created in the image of God. I am no longer "my own man" or "my own woman"; I am Christ's person.

No disciple will arrive at full Christ-consciousness on this side of the grave. We will not be completed until God completes us in our death and in eternal life. Thomas Troeger writes,

> "The moist fingers of the Spirit which first molded the clay vessels of our bodies are every day reshaping our hearts and minds. God's skilled hands know every contour of our being. They keep smoothing the rough surfaces of our hatred and repairing the cracks caused by tragedy and despair. And when we die, those same confident hands shall turn again the potter's wheel and refashion who we are into what we ought to be."[1]

Likewise Paul wrote to the Philippians, "I am quite certain that the

One who began this good work in you will see that it is finished when the Day of Christ Jesus comes" (Philippians 1:6, *The Jerusalem Bible*).

We are never finally converted until God converts us on the far side of the grave; that is the hope we hold in Christ. Our earthbound bodies will never bear full Christ-consciousness, and until that day when we are released from our human limitations, we will always be tempted to put self-consciousness ahead of Christ.

Time: A Context for Conversion

Who is responsible for conversion and when does it occur? We do not and, indeed, cannot convert ourselves; we are too self-centered for that. God converts; as Paul said to the Corinthians, "I planted the seed, and Apollos watered it; but God made it grow" (1 Corinthians 3:6-7, NEB). Conversion is divine action taken at divine instigation. And while God does not ride roughshod over us, for we must ultimately respond, God does determine the appropriate time. It is God who calls upon our receptivity to transform us into Christ-consciousness.

Emilie Griffin explains her own conversion experience in this way.

> When I first began to experience the power of God in my own life, I could hardly believe it. Something very real and discernible was happening to me, yet I felt it could not or should not be happening. God was speaking to me; God was calling me. He spoke no louder than a whisper, but I heard him. And each time that I heard him, and chose him, a change occurred, the opening of a door I had not guessed was there. . . . It was conversion.[2]

But when does conversion occur? Many people assume that conversion is a one-time decision that brings permanent and final change. That is a woefully narrow assumption. For many of us, there is a point in our lives when we do make a first-time converting decision to be conscious of Christ's leadership in our lives. But it is not a one-time-only decision. George Gallup, Jr., and David Poling articulate this well in their book *The Search for America's Faith:*

> Christianity is a growth process. One monastery that flourished in the Middle Ages was known for a phrase with which the community began each day. Their phrase was, "Let us begin again to be Christians." It may be that in our own time too much emphasis has been

placed on the "day that I found Christ" rather than the "day after." Christian conversion is the beginning but hardly the conclusion for those serious about becoming full and complete in the Lord.[3]

John McCall, a contemporary psychologist, calls conversion "the essence of the Christian vocation." He adds that "conversion is never once and for all; it's a process, a continuing series of events."[4] Avery Dulles, the distinguished Roman Catholic theologian, talks of his surprise to learn that his "conversion had scarcely begun" upon his first decision.[5] C. S. Lewis commented that Christian growth happens "everytime you make a choice . . . all your life long,"[6] and Karl Barth speaks of the "coexistence" of the old and new person, even after conversion.[7] But Thomas Merton, who spent a lifetime in contemplation, says it most clearly, "We are not converted only once in our lives, but many times; and this endless series of large and small conversions, inner revolutions, leads to our transformation in Christ."[8]

Evangelism, Nurture, and a Process for Conversion

John Westerhoff says that "evangelism . . . refers to the process by which the Christian community of faith, through the proclamation of the Gospel in word and deed, leads persons inside and outside the church to a radical reorientation of life—conversion."[9] Evangelism is the church's task of encouraging persons to make converting decisions for Jesus Christ—first-time decisions as well as ongoing decisions. While most young people are at a point of making first-time decisions for conversion, the challenge with youth is to help them see that a first-time decision is important only as the first of many decisions.

Many junior high youth are developmentally able to make that first decision, and the church should affirm them as they do so. The church's formal affirmation of that decision is the act of baptism or confirmation, depending upon its tradition. Most junior high youth are not, however, mature enough to make *onetime* decisions of any kind. They can launch their faith in a particular direction and they can express a desire to belong, but seventh grade youth should not be asked to overcome their self-consciousness. They cannot be asked to skip the developmental paradox of adolescence. The junior high faith decision is primarily a directional one. Junior high youth are well served when this is interpreted to them.

Clear models of this continuing conversion process are needed.

If youth can see in the lives of adults that a first converting decision will lead to many more future conversions, they will be better equipped to continue their faith journeys. There is no more appealing evangelistic witness than for youth to see other "first-timers" making faith decisions and also to see parents, pastors, and youth leaders being more fully converted to Christ.

We are witnesses to youth not only because Christ once saved us but because Christ continually saves and converts us. The appropriate invitation from Christian adults to young people reaching for faith is not "Come and make the decision for Christ that I made years ago." Rather, the message needs to be "Come and make a decision for faith even as I am also making one at this point in my life." Of course, adults and youth will be at different levels of discipleship, but God is converting both to a deeper consciousness of Christ.

What, then, is nurture? Nurture is also a task of the church; persons cannot nurture themselves. While it has similarities to the task of evangelism, nurture is actually a quite different task. Nurture is a task of formation. It provides faith traditions, stories, and memories which contribute to building a faith heritage. Nurture provides the raw material out of which conversion eventually arises. A person is not converted in a vacuum. In some way, when a person is converted, he or she has been nurtured toward that conversion. While conversion is what God does, nurture is what the community of the faithful does, year after year after year.

Nurture and evangelism, then, are closely intertwined activities of the church. They represent two ways in which adults can be faith advocates for youth. One approach is to bring faith *near* to youth; this is the nurturing role. It happens often in subtle ways and does not require a decisional response. We bring faith near to youth when they experience the traditions, relationships, and stories of a nurturing community. The other approach is to bring faith *directly* to youth; this is the evangelizing role. The second approach takes a more potent stance and does require a decisional response. We bring faith directly to youth when they encounter a crossroad that offers a converting decision. In both cases we are faith advocates, and we must consciously perform both roles. Faith must be brought to young people both nearly and directly, both by nurture and evangelism.[10]

The adjacent chart describes the church's twin tasks of nurture and evangelism with youth.

THE CHURCH'S TASKS OF EVANGELISM AND NURTURE

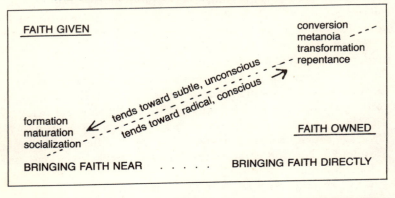

NURTURE . . . THE CHURCH'S TASKS . . . EVANGELISM

What actually happens to the person in conversion? We have affirmed the fact that conversion is decisional. God first acts and invites; the church nurtures and evangelizes; but it is the person's task to respond, and respond continually. Conversion in the life of a believer is initiated by a decision for faith and is continued by subsequent faith decisions. My conversions are not something for which I can plan. I cannot say to myself, "I will be converted tomorrow!" But even if conversion often happens without personal intent, I can decide at what point I will be receptive to God's converting action.

We rarely anticipate God's invitation. We often do not welcome it. But our response will be a conscious decision. It is doubtful that an unconscious conversion is possible. The converted person may not be fully aware of the ramifications of a decision nor of the direction in which it will lead. But that person is aware that he or she has stood at a crossroads, with one path leading toward fuller consciousness of Christ; and this was the path that was chosen.

Conversion requires saying no as well as saying yes. It requires endings as well as beginnings. Because it is decisional, it is optional. People can decide for something else. The adolescent can decide to remain self-conscious. In conversion we die to one thing in order to be born to another. Conversion is that decisional point at which we experience death and resurrection into a more faithful way of being.

There is a sequential process for persons experiencing conversion. The sequence can repeat itself over and over again because persons are in continuous need of conversion. (See the chart "The Conversion Process of Christians.")

THE CONVERSION PROCESS OF CHRISTIANS

(the sequence through which persons are converted throughout their lives)

CONTENTMENT
▯
"I'm satisfied with things as they are; life is 'normal,' routine, happy, contented; I do not feel challenged or threatened."

INTERRUPTION
▯
"The Spirit interrupts my contentment. I feel stirred, challenged, upset, made uncomfortable by something, some force or person, some idea or problem or vision or feeling. The Spirit disturbs me."

WRESTLE
▯
"Either a brief pause, or a long struggle in which I attempt to fight off the Spirit's interruption. I see it as a nuisance, a troubling presence. I avoid it; or I may fight it openly."

SEARCH
▯
"I begin to give in, to find out more. I'm seeking, striving. I have a great openness and vulnerability to the Spirit and its leadership. Out of a time of restlessness, often a new image comes to me. I may not yet be able to describe or explain what this means. It may be more intuitive."

CONVERSION DECISION
▯
"The call of the Spirit now becomes more definite. I may be very emotional and idealistic. But the converting decision tends to have a strong forward thrust to it that moves me along a great adventure. Faced with the definite choice, I make a decision to follow the leading of the Spirit. The decision may seem easy and natural, or it may continue to feel difficult and painful. The decision may be so positive that I am temporarily blinded to its costs or its limitations."

ASSIMILATION
▯
"I am now faced with this new conversion decision, and how to assimilate it into my life-style and into my former patterns of living and 'faithing.' Pain and discomfort can certainly be felt at this time. It is often a time of being realistic, of compromising, adjusting, trimming. I must incorporate the new decision. It must become 'me.'"

CONTENTMENT
▯
"Full cycle, back again to the ease and satisfaction of the conversion incorporated in my life and faith."

At any point in this sequence, persons can and do retreat from the process, thwarting real conversion. Persons often linger at one particular point or another. One man, in my pastoral experience, has been stuck at the wrestling stage for twenty years; his argument with God has never been resolved. Other persons may, typically, wrestle and surrender as they make the converting decision and then assume that the process is all finished. Some may take days or weeks or years to be converted to Christ–consciousness in just one dimension of their lives. Adults who have been on a lifelong journey of faith may work through this process many times. Youth will learn this conversion cycle by trial and error. They will need experienced guides for the journey.

The Title of a Conversion

The story of your conversion does have a title. If you do have a story to tell, then there is a title that proclaims its distinctiveness. The story of your converting journey is your testimony. The story is much more than just how God saved you at one point in your life. That is but one episode in the story. The story has a much deeper plot and has many more climaxes, interludes, crises, valleys, and mountaintops. The story of your conversion is the continuing story of how God is bringing you to a deeper consciousness of Christ. Colossians 1:27 (TEV) affirms that "God's plan is to make known his secret to his people, this rich and glorious secret which he has for all peoples. And the secret is that Christ is in you. . . ."

Let me share a recent conversion to Jesus Christ. I am a person who finds great joy in my work, but my work can be an addiction. The problem of workaholics like me is that we are convinced that our worth as persons is wrapped up in our ability to produce. We believe that we are worthy only if we achieve. There are degrees of being a workaholic, and mine does not seem fatal, but I have always been convinced that there is no limit to my energy. However, recently I made a discovery that startled me. I realized that there *are* definite limits to my energy and to what I can accomplish.

I became a father in the midst of working on a doctorate and holding down a demanding job. With the added responsibilities of developing this manuscript, I found that I had taken on far too much. Yet I could not and would not admit failure or limitation. Relaxation and personal time vanished. Every minute became task-oriented. And my ego and I went "thud." For a person who has had a seemingly boundless supply of energy, that was a very frightening experience. Of course, in my head I've always known that there are limits to anyone's time and commitment. But for myself,

I had always felt that I could take on whatever I desired. What I experienced was likely an early sign of midlife crisis, which most people experience—a painful realization of one's limits, one's short-age of time and energy and accomplishment. When my wife mentioned what a price I was paying for overextending myself, the lights blinked on and I took a hard look at what I had been avoiding all summer.

I experienced a conversion when I saw that Christ was not contained in my frantic efforts of ministry but was beyond these efforts. When I became aware that I could not take on the entire world, I became aware that Christ's call was for me to *do* less in his name and to enjoy more. I still have not fully incorporated this conversion into my life, for I have spent three decades establishing this very bad habit of trying to exceed my limits. But my eyes have been opened and I can see Christ in a deeper dimension. That has been a recent experience of my conversion. Let me now share the story of the title of my conversion.

I grew up in a very active Baptist family. I was baptized at eight or nine. I don't recall the exact age. It was a fairly minor experience of conversion. Merely being born into my family meant being born into a spiritual environment.

But as a young adult I found that something was different. In my sophomore year in college, I was well into the faith-shaping task of separation.[11] I wanted distance between myself and my faith tradition. I wanted no part of my Baptist upbringing. I was determined to be a city planner, perhaps a politician. I had gifts in that field, and I loved it. I excelled in my small college's political science department. I was active in alternative campus Christian groups, but I disliked the institutional church and I particularly disliked pastors.

For no apparent cause, in the middle of that year a deep restlessness came over me. In late winter of 1968 I began to wrestle with God. Sleepless nights followed. *What was the matter?* I wondered. Girls? Self-image? Homework? Friends? I really knew what it was. I knew God wanted my attention, and yet I didn't want to know what God wanted. But the situation grew more intense. My sleepless nights had me walking outside through the early morning hours.

I finally realized the meaning of the title of the Broadway musical *Your Arms Too Short to Box with God.* And so one evening, feeling very strange, I spoke to God, "OK, God, what do you want? You've got my attention. I haven't been able to sleep, eat, go to classes, relate. You've wrecked my last two weeks!" No lightning flashed; no thunder roared; but the message was clearer than it had ever been before: God was calling me to pastoral ministry. My response was swift: "No way!" My self-image simply would not allow it. My friends would laugh me off campus.

So, I offered a compromise. I would be a very good Christian politician. I would work for God in a secular arena. But the response was "NO WAY!"—and this time it was God communicating! Pastoral ministry was the calling. I was embarrassed to be called to pastoral ministry. I avoided God and chaplains and anyone else who "looked Christian" for the next week!

I remember feeling violently shaken, as though God had grabbed me by the shirt and shaken me until my head wobbled. I was physically weak. Finally, early one morning, staggering around in an isolated area of the campus, the time came. "OK, Lord, I can't take this any longer. What do you really want?" In the moments that followed, in nonverbal communication, God and I negotiated! God was calling me to pastoral ministry, but it would be a unique ministry: I could be me. I wouldn't have to pretend to be anyone else. In fact, that was what God wanted; that felt good. And I would be a layman; I was not being called to anything else. Finally it came, I was called to be a layman and a pastor—a lay pastor. Was there such a thing? I had no idea. I only knew that was my call. Today, I still am called by that converting experience—as a lay pastor.

And my conversion journey has, since that day, taken many ups and downs, many more converting decisions, many more reluctant experiences in which I was made more conscious of Christ. But each experience has reflected and deepened that call which still permeates my life, my vocation, and the meaning of my faith. Indeed, the recent conversion experience I related to you of being aware of my limits is connected to my unfolding ministry. I'm learning that my call isn't to work myself to death. And so my conversion-journey is entitled "Shaped by a Call."

If you were to write your conversion experiences, what would be the title? What would be the central theme? What unifying thread has connected God's activity in your life? If your conversion to Jesus Christ has a title, what would it communicate? Could you tell another person about the stories of your conversion? Would you tell an adolescent about the ways you are being converted to Jesus Christ?

Youth need to hear our ongoing stories. If we had better handles on God's converting actions in our lives, we would be stronger witnesses with our youth. We are not capable of converting young people. No matter how much love or regard we have for them, we cannot convert them. But our love and regard surely can be used by God, as the Spirit works its converting way into their lives and into our own.

FOR REFLECTION

1. Identify several particular moments of conversion or emerging Christ-consciousness in your own life. Can you discover a pattern revealed in the way God calls you and in the way you respond? How might you characterize this pattern? What title might you attach to it?

2. How might you be able to share these moments of conversion with young people you know? Make three lists. One will be of people to share with; the second will be of appropriate settings in which to share with a particular person (at the church, at the school, at a fast-food restaurant, at a ball game); and the third will be of techniques for telling the story (some will be merely suggestive, nurturing techniques; others will be more direct). Begin to strategize and make the necessary contacts. Is this a new way for you to think about evangelizing? In what sense?

7

Culture-Shaping Evangelism

Wendy Ryan reported the following story from the experience of medical missionary Dr. Daniel Fountain.[1] It is the inspiring and tragic story of a man named Mapela, who lived in a village near Vanga in Zaire. Mapela was a bright and engaging person who, although struck with polio when very young and left with severe leg problems, had managed to continue in school and to maintain a positive spirit. Because of his perseverance in struggling to school on homemade crutches and his determination to be a helpful member of his society, he attracted the attention of American friends. These friends helped pay for his education and eventually arranged for surgical help for him. After two very difficult operations and five long months of rehabilitation, and wearing a pair of special shoes sent from Nairobi, Mapela was able to walk, to go home, and to begin a new life for others. But within two years he was dead from the malnutrition that was part of daily life in his village.

This story reads like a parable on the need for cultural salvation. Mapela had been saved; his culture had not. His life potential was lost in the brokenness of the culture to which he returned.

Some people are convinced that the only way to save the world is to save individual persons one by one. Certainly that is one legitimate way to save the world, but after reading this story, I am even more convinced that the gospel calls us not only to individual salvation but also to a cultural salvation.

Jesus wanted to evangelize culture. This was his most remarkable and predominant teaching. His vision was to evangelize culture by introducing the kingdom of God on earth . . . a "Kingdom Culture"! While Jesus did advocate preaching the gospel to persons one by one, he talked even more about introducing the kingdom of God in the world.

Evangelism as a Personal and Cultural Invitation to the Kingdom of God

Evangelism is a personal invitation to become part of God's kingdom—not only to *belong* to the kingdom but to help build it and make it a reality on earth. Many recent studies show that the personal invitation works better within established relationships than between strangers. Young people can identify their friends and peers and can issue personal invitations to belong to God's kingdom.

But evangelism is also a cultural invitation to the kingdom of God. It is to "invite" your culture to be more Christlike, more Christ-centered, more like the kingdom of God. That is the reality we seek. That is the vision we need to share with our world.

It isn't enough to evangelize young people one by one. We must also evangelize their culture. Culture shaping isn't something that we adults can do *for* youth, but it is something we can enable them to do for themselves. As advisors, pastors, and workers with youth, we seek to evangelize by shaping with adolescents the culture in which they live and mature. We seek a culture permeated with Christ-consciousness.

This is the vision which Paul shared with the Ephesians: "[God] has made known to us his hidden purpose—to be put into effect when the time was ripe: namely, that the universe, all in heaven and on earth, might be brought into a unity in Christ" (Ephesians 1:9-10, NEB). And again, in the Gospel of John, "It was not to judge the world that God sent his Son into the world, but that through him the *world* might be saved" (John 3:17, NEB, author's emphasis). Through Christ, the world of youth can be saved; Christ can and will save not only young persons but also their culture.

We need to explore with more care this whole idea of young people and their culture. Ross Snyder has pointed out:

> *Human* beings live in a culture, not just a "natural" world. Each of us is a *self-in-culture*, not just a self. . . .
> Too long we have acted as if each young person *all by himself* could

make up his mind, choose a life style, establish a life world. If only we poured into him enough facts and admonitions and kept him frantically busy. . . . Actually he can make up his mind, establish a style of life and life world only *as he is a member of a culture*. . . . Youth is the time to begin . . . creating culture rather than consuming and conforming to the culture other people apart from him make.[2]

Youth are persons–in–culture, and salvation may not call them to authentic conversion if the call does not include their culture. Salvation will have more influence as we enable young persons to work out salvation (Philippians 2:12) within their culture. Youth peer culture can be redeemed. Indeed, youth culture is already being redeemed and saved. We can choose to be a part of God's saving activity in youth culture, or we can ignore it.

Amish, Shakers, and other religious sects believe that the only way to evangelize culture is to avoid contact with any adversity or pluralism, and therefore create their own culture. A person's religious community becomes, then, his or her total world. Some people of the religious right today attempt the same goal with their Christian schools, Christian TV and radio networks, and Christian Yellow Pages. They try to make it possible to live in an urban society and yet avoid contact with that which is alien to their belief system. But such approaches deny God our efforts in helping to redeem "the universe, all in heaven and on earth," bringing a new "unity in Christ" (Ephesians 1:10, NEB). We deny God our help in the divine plan "that through him [Christ] the world might be saved" (John 3:17, NEB).

Christians need not run from a pluralistic society. Indeed we must not deceive ourselves into thinking that we know which groups or causes or places or ideas God uses for divine purposes. For example, at the beginning of his work, most Christians in America would have avoided identification with Martin Luther King, Jr. But now, with clear hindsight, many acknowledge that Christ was in King's efforts, bringing about a vision of the kingdom in which there is no male, no female, no black, no white, no enslaved or oppressed. Thomas Troeger says,

To accept Jesus as our Savior is to receive the strength to face the world. . . . It is the commitment of disciples who embrace their Lord by reaching out to the world.
Christ is no longer simply "*my* Savior." Such a claim treats Christ as though he were a private possession. . . .

An individual's decision to accept Christ means to recognize Christ as the *world's* Savior. . . .[3]

As people deeply concerned with youth ministry, we are involved in shaping youth culture. It is a task in which nearly every person who cares about youth is already engaged, with or without conscious intent. For we are involved not just in impacting youth, but in empowering them to affect their own culture. We find ways to affirm those things in youth peer culture that are Christ-worthy, and we continuously suggest alternatives for those things which we consider destructive. As youth seek our advice about legitimate ways they can participate in their culture and remain faithful to Christ, they are seeking from us counsel as cultural evangelists. Such counsel can have a powerful influence on a young person's participation in peer culture.

Christian youth can be more than consumers. They can be a part of Christ's transforming activity in their culture. The active youth in a church spend only a fraction of their time in the church or its fellowship—maybe no more than four hours a week—yet that time often wields a significant, disproportionate influence in their lives. Because of the direction and strength they find, they are often able, in rather remarkable ways, to be strong in the face of evil, to be mature in the face of destructive options, to be responsible about their future in the face of dead ends, and to affirm life as hopeful persons. Youth who have yet to work through the obstacle of self-consciousness will most likely not be social prophets confronting their peers in the halls of the schools, but this is not the cultural witness we seek anyway! The quiet, subtle, and humble actions of Christian youth in their culture often accomplish more culture shaping than noisy actions or loud demonstrations. The urge to conform to peers is strong in adolescent culture; any deviation, based on quiet but sincere motives, is a significant witness.

What does a culture-shaping witness look like? Traditionally, we have asked church-related youth to take negative stands in their culture: not to dance, or smoke, or drink, or have sexual intercourse outside of marriage. We can, however, also ask young people to position themselves in their culture in positive ways: to befriend the lonely and the ridiculed, to build relationships with those of different cultures or races, to represent honesty and truthfulness and a sense of Christian vocation. We should urge Christian youth to participate in their peer culture, to be a part of it, to claim it, to transform it.

Actually, we encourage adults to do the same thing by participating in American culture. Yes, our culture is male dominated, racially exclusive, materialistic, militaristic, filled with options to get away and avoid responsibility, but that is precisely where Christian adults belong—standing within their culture trying to evangelize it, trying to redeem it, trying to make Christ realizable in the midst of it.

The Task of Culture Shaping

The evangelistic task of culture shaping with youth involves at least three functions.

The first is to help young people recognize Christ in their culture. The evangelistic task is to point out Christ in other people, in world events, in their own experiences, in their culture. Christ isn't locked up in the church or in stained glass windows or in the private soul of the believer. Christ is already a part of youth culture, and our task is to help youth see Christ there. "The Word had life in himself and this life brought light to men. The light shines in the darkness, and the darkness has never put it out" (John 1:4-5, TEV).

The second function is to help young people shape their culture to be more Christlike. To be merely reluctant recipients of popular culture or to avoid contact with peer culture is not the task of young Christians. An evangelistic question for youth is "How can I make my culture more Christlike?" In the fourth chapter of Luke, Jesus began his public ministry by announcing to the Nazarenes what he intended to do in his Galilean culture: "to announce good news to the poor, to proclaim release for prisoners and recovery of sight for the blind . . ." (Luke 4:18, NEB). When we begin to shape our culture as Christians, these become our goals as well. Justice and liberation become our themes.

The third function is to develop peer ministry in the church as a legitimate, Christ-filled expression of youth culture. Youth culture is not just something "out there," created by disc jockeys and television. It is whatever and wherever youth create it. In your church's peer ministry, do youth claim and recognize the culture that is there as their own, or is it adult-dominated? Youth peer culture expressed in the church can help youth experiment with how to be faithful in today's world.

The Personal Invitation to the Gospel

We will now examine some specific and practical ideas on how we can extend to youth the personal invitation to the gospel.

To reach more young persons with the gospel, it may be essential to offer different kinds of opportunities for their involvement in our churches. Most youth classes and groups will not exceed twenty persons in regular attendance because youth are seeking a sense of belonging, which can more often be found in small groups. We can extend outreach by a wide range of activities offered as choices to youth. There are notable exceptions to the twenty-person limit, but they tend to be just that—exceptions.

Adults and active youth can express a real ministry of concern to those who are marginally active. It involves letting these youth know that we care when they are not with us, that we are diminished by their absence. Christian love is accountable, and we affirm this whenever we take seriously a person's presence or absence and follow up on it. Immediate follow-up on absent youth who have attended regularly is important. In these ways we extend a personal invitation to participate in Christian community.

There are no special tricks to reaching young persons who are not involved. Friend-to-friend invitations have always proved to be the most effective method. As young people participate in their culture, they undoubtedly have contact with youth outside the church. Inviting them to activities, retreats, and fellowship events is the most effective way of reaching out. Encouraging youth to do this is an obvious evangelistic task. Youth groups that meet only on Sunday mornings and evenings in restricted groupings will not have as many opportunities for their members to reach out to friends as will groups that engage in retreats, trips, and other special events. Choirs, classes, fellowship activities, retreats, and mission trips must be defined as inclusive or open fellowships rather than exclusive cliques. Training adult workers and youth themselves to be conscious of this should be an evangelistic priority in our churches.

Often we can reach entire families through young persons who become active in our church youth groups, but this requires special effort and intentional follow-up. Youth peer groups in the church can be inviting and welcoming communities. Youth and their adult leaders can be trained to identify, invite, welcome, and incorporate those who are unreached by the gospel.

Evangelism is not only for the unreached, but for the reaching. Every active young person in our churches is among those reaching toward Christ's full stature. If our churches want to have an impact on the faith of our active, reaching youth, then our first priority must be a carefully conceived discipleship plan. It needs to be a plan that communicates the fact that discipleship nurture is not just for those becoming members but for all youth. If your church is one with a narrow conception of discipleship nurture—in which you have a pastor's class during Lent, receive the students into membership on Palm Sunday, and feel you're finished—correct that mistake.

If you are not nurturing the active youth who are reaching for faith, then don't worry over the unreached youth. Make certain you are nurturing the reaching youth, and then include the unreached.

I have an increasing concern for the style of our personal invitation to older senior high youth and young adults. This group of sixteen- to twenty-four-year-olds is the one we fail most consistently. There are seven faith-shaping tasks on which young persons must work as they reach for faith.[4]

1. *Experiencing:* spiritual emotions, religious feelings, sacred experiences.
2. *Categorizing:* sorting out and consolidating one's religious experiences; making sense of the experiences in understandable terms.
3. *Choosing:* deciding what is true and important.
4. *Claiming:* the act of commitment; conversion; giving one's life to something.
5. *Deepening:* the act of maturing in one's faith commitments
6. *Separating:* pulling away from earlier convictions and decisions; giving oneself space for reflection and consolidation; rebellion.
7. *Responding:* gaining a sense of one's life calling; discovering your own giftedness.

It is in the sixth and seventh tasks that we most often fail our youth. The sixth task, that of separating, legitimizes the need for space and distance from the church which many young adults need. We must not lay guilt on them but must continue to communicate our concern as they work through this faith task.

The seventh and final task is that of responding with openness to a life calling or a vocation. We often fail to offer a theology of vocation, of gifts and callings. To counter that failing I would suggest that one evangelistic response might be for churches, associations, and national denominations to offer more internships for older youth and young adults. Through such internships they could experience Christian ministry as vocation. Options for short- and long-term training and service, for which young persons would be paid, could provide opportunities to take their faith to its fullest expression. Because I feel this is so important, allow me to cite three illustrations:

1. I met my wife when we were hired to be summer interns for an urban church in Kansas City, Missouri. Our job was to operate their inner-city recreational ministry with children and youth. For us, it was a special opportunity to try out our gifts and to put our ideas of ministry to work. The intent was not necessarily to prepare us for pastoral ministry but to prepare us for lifelong service in whatever form that would take.

2. "The Missioners" were eight young persons employed by the First Baptist Church of Dayton, Ohio, to sing, act, perform, and interact with persons in various institutions in Dayton, as well as in public places. In the eight weeks of the project, they went to nursing homes, jails, homes for the mentally retarded, veterans' hospitals, children's centers, vacation Bible schools, public plazas, and senior citizen nutrition sites. By summer's end they had proclaimed the gospel to over four thousand persons in seventy different settings. But just as importantly, these young persons had been exposed to ministry as vocation, and the church had been able to give meaningful employment to persons who might otherwise have found only unsatisfying entry-level jobs in the fast-food business.

3. George Gallup, the pollster, found this in his research on youth and young adults:

> The urge of young people to serve may be expressed both within the religious fellowship and beyond the church. While many caring young members will not enter the ministry as a full-time vocation, a significant number may wish to become paraclergy. . . . Recently a United Methodist minister . . . hired several college students in his church to do hospital and shut-in calling during their Christmas vacation. The impact upon the sick, the shut-in, and the disabled was astounding.[5]

The Cultural Invitation to the Gospel

Now allow me to offer four possible ways to extend to youth a cultural invitation to the gospel.

1. In my church's youth fellowship group, we engage every other year in a project that our youth eagerly anticipate: a youth mission exchange trip. We contact a church within one day's drive and negotiate with them to spend four or five days in their community, and we invite them to spend a similar length of time in our city. The purpose of the exchange trips is for youth to be able to recognize Christ at work in other communities, through another church, through a specific mission project, and through new peer friendships. Instead of engaging in a mission trip in which we go to serve others, we learn through this approach that mission is mutual. Junior high and senior high youth have few opportunities to experience life in new settings in different homes and communities. The newness of the setting makes it easier for them to identify Christ in the community and in people's lives than is possible back home in more familiar settings. In addition they learn a great deal about their own situation when they host the returning group.

2. Another cultural invitation to the gospel can be found in interracial events. We may not always be able to integrate our churches, but we certainly can engage in interracial events with black, white, Hispanic, Asian and American Indian churches. Through such events we can recognize how Christ works in the world, and we can build bridges of understanding rather than walls of prejudice. I highly recommend bringing two churches together for more than a token, one-time event. Youth from my church and youth from a National Baptist church in our city met for a long-term service project, which concluded with a joint celebration.

3. To the extent that the peer ministry in your church is a legitimate expression by youth of their own youth culture, and to the extent that this youth culture is an expression of Christ, you are extending a cultural invitation to the gospel with youth. If your peer ministry is not Christ-centered but, rather, centered around something more superficial, then there is obvious evangelistic work to be done. If your youth ministry represents adult culture more than that of youth, then you also have an evangelistic task.

The longer I engage in youth ministry, the more convinced I become about the importance of youth providing their own leadership for their activities. I am convinced that the role of the adult in youth ministry is to be an enabler—to help youth do what they choose to do and to be an affirming presence for the youth, as well as for the gospel.

4. Another cultural invitation to the gospel involves the parents of youth. Parents must obviously be reached if we are to reach youth. We need to communicate with parents the importance of faith nurturing in the church and in the home. I have, for example, started the tradition of writing a letter to parents of incoming seventh graders, stressing the unique influence they now have to point the attention of their son or daughter to our church's youth ministry. The parents have related to me that this contact helped them to be much more alert and supportive. The pressures on parents are great, and often the reminder is helpful. Faith is the foundation for everything that parents hope will come to their children. Without the foundation of a mature faith, marriages, vocations, skills, friendships, and success will amount to little. Parents do have a cultural contribution to offer to their young people. They can be supportive of peer culture as it occurs in the church, and they can be supportive of their own children as they participate in peer culture in the larger society. But parents need consistent training and support if that is to occur.

In conclusion, if you feel called to evangelize with youth but miss the opportunity to engage youth in culture shaping, then you cannot live up to your calling.

Evangelism is an invitational activity. To be effective evangelists with youth, we must extend both a personal and a cultural invitation to the kingdom of God and the redeeming love that is Jesus Christ.

FOR REFLECTION

1. Brainstorm the ways youth in your church are already engaged in culture shaping. Are they engaged in culture shaping intentionally or by chance? How can you help them put such activities into the context of raising the Christ-consciousness in their culture? What are some specific ways you can help your youth engage in culture shaping which they are not doing now?

2. Can peer pressure, parental pressure, or moral pressure play positive roles in the culture-shaping process for youth? In which specific ways?

3. Can you think of twenty specific ways that youth can witness positively to their culture with the help of the church?

8

God's Time—The Right Time

The question of timing is a crucial question to the evangelist with youth. The Greek language of the New Testament had two words for our word "time." The word *chronos* is the source of our word "chronology" and is a word that measures time quantitatively. Chronos refers to a marking or measuring of time; its function can be seen in a phrase like "it took a long time to do it."

The second Greek word for time was *kairos*. It is a word which marks those times that have a special quality. Its function can be seen in phrases like "it's the right time" or "now is the time of salvation." *Kairos* means a favorable time, a time of special opportunity, a time in a person's life for God-given possibility to become actualized. It is the time of readiness for something to happen.

The Right Time—A Particular Story

The young woman speaking had just completed a study of adolescent faith development. She was reflecting on her own particular faith journey. Listen to her witness of how *kairos* worked at various times in her experience.

"When I was in junior high school, I attended church regularly because that was something my family did together. I remember sitting in my Sunday school class and talking with my teacher about trying to get along with my brother. I came away feeling I should be nicer to him. She [my teacher] was a very sweet, soft-spoken lady who modeled what I believed Christianity should be about.

"At my home, which I thought was a good Christian home, we often prayed at dinner and before bed. My father was the closest example I could think of to the ideal Christian—soft-spoken, patient, gentle, forgiving, and loving. I remember once telling him that I did not think a man in our church was a Christian because he had said something unkind. My father gently said to me, 'Who put you in the judgment seat?' Wow, what an impact he had on me.

"My mother, on the other hand, was in charge of disciplining us. She told us we had to go to church because it meant so much to our father. While we never talked about Christ in our home, I did believe that Christian morality and going to church were important. I was baptized when I was eight years old.

"By ninth grade, I began to see hypocrisy in people at church and especially among the members of the youth group. They talked about loving others, but they were very prejudiced. I remember inviting my girlfriend, who was Jewish, to B.Y.F., and the kids began to tell jokes about Jews in front of her. I decided that the church, Christianity, and the whole bit was for the birds! I would not return.

"Throughout my high school and college years, I experimented with other values and other religions. My boyfriend in high school was Jewish, and I became very interested in Judaism. His family invited me to participate in Passover meals, as well as many other Jewish services. I had many questions about Jewish history and the concentration camps, which his father was glad to answer. As time went on, I became interested in other philosophies. I took Chinese philosophy in college and became friendly with my professor. I began to believe that Zen Buddhism was really the way. I had many spiritual experiences as I learned to meditate. However, eventually, I rejected Zen, also. I could never strive for nothingness.

"My college days ended and my religious searching had left me nowhere. I had a very empty feeling. It seemed like nothing mattered. It was at this time that the gospel of Jesus Christ was presented to me in a new way. It was as if I had never heard it before. I tried to find the loopholes, but I finally became convinced that this was fundamentally different because it brought new meaning to my life. I became busy shaping my faith all over again. I still am. When

I accepted Christ, I felt that I had something my parents and the church of my childhood never experienced. But now I am finally reaching the point where I can see that many of the things they value as a part of their faith, I value in my own faith, too."

This story, while unique in some ways, is also very typical. The journey of faith development is amazing in the way it comes together and falls apart and comes together again. No one could have predicted the directions that this particular person's faith would move—from junior high through her college years—as the occasions of *kairos* presented themselves. No one knows where she will finally arrive, nor where her religious quest will lead her now. She is just beginning to understand that *kairos* (a time of special opportunity) comes more than once. Her ability to understand and articulate her own faith development will serve her well in the future.

It was not the times of security and contentment along this young woman's journey which caused her to search for a meaningful faith. It was her moments of insecurity and questioning that motivated her search, and brought on the "right" time.

Adolescence—The Right Time for Evangelism

In the unfolding of faith, one of God's richest times is the period of adolescence. These years are the favorable times to experience the rich feelings of the Spirit, to experiment letting go of ourselves and our self-consciousness, to pour ourselves out for others. This is *kairos* time—the right time.

There are, I believe, at least four reasons why evangelism is a fruitful concern for ministry with adolescents.

1. The more secure the person, the more protected the person becomes from questions and questing. Secure persons are less prone to take risks or to ask faith questions. Adults often experience crises of faith during occasional periods of insecurity. The teen years generally tend to be times of immense personal insecurity. There are so many changes—physically, sexually, relationally, emotionally, intellectually—that teens are not yet sure of themselves or the world around them.

Adult life can often become encrusted with a false sense of security that inhibits a reaching for faith. But, ordinarily, adolescent years are not walled in by patterns of false security. The insecurity of youth is a receptive environment for faith shaping. Therefore, these years may be among the most spiritually active.

2. The more complicated the life, the more difficult to change. When you are encumbered by a long-term career, family responsibility, house and car payments, etc., change has to be carefully considered. Experiments must be weighed with caution.

For youth, the simplicity in their interpersonal networks often enables them to ask faith questions, to try new ideas and behaviors, to be idealistic, to develop a creative imagination.

3. With little to lose and often lacking adult notions of propriety and formality, youth can be incisive. They can cut straight through to the heart of an issue. They waste no words. They can say what they are thinking—to the point of bluntness. Often they can lift up what is fundamentally important, stripping away the trivial and the unnecessary.

4. Adolescence is the intersection of the need to affiliate and the need to personalize. Youth are often ambivalent in wanting to belong (true of most junior high youth) and in wanting to personalize faith (true of most senior high youth and young adults). Youth are often saying, "I want to belong to a faith community that allows me the freedom to make of The Faith, my own faith." Adolescence is the most predictable time of passover from belonging to personalizing.

George Gallup, Jr., analyzing the results of a significant survey of the religious attitudes of American youth, summarizes this way:

> If the . . . churches are serious about the complaints and cries of youth, they will find themselves entering into a whole new period of program, attention, and care of the young around them. . . .
>
> Each congregation should endeavor to have a special ministry or ministries to teenagers. Right now too many churches have virtually ignored this age group. . . . A true ministry to teenagers will never wait for them to appear at the church door, rather it will reach out to this age group wherever they are to be found. . . .
>
> Spiritual nourishment is one of the highest goals that young people presently have in their formative lives. Ironic that they should be telling the churches that they have great spiritual needs and aspirations. The young indicate that they want to go deep into the great places of God through prayer, Bible study, and personal discipline.[1]

Within each person is a unique and distinctive rhythm that determines our unfolding as persons. Particular aspects of this rhythm are magnified at special times in life. At these times, adolescents, like adults, experience stirrings within themselves that are divinely given. In adolescence and adulthood, the Spirit uses these times to interrupt our contentment and move us toward conversion. *Human development, then, is really God's timing, God's* kairos. When we think of the needs and cries of today's youth, the words of Paul become ever more clear: "Now is the favorable time; this is the day of salvation" (2 Corinthians 6:2, *The Jerusalem Bible*).

Faith and Insecurity

The close relationship between faith and insecurity reinforces the idea that adolescence is indeed God's time and points to the need for genuine faith models and courageous evangelists.

There is today a popular misconception about the role that faith plays in human life. Many people assume that having faith means being certain and assured. They believe that faith is the solid rock, the anchor, something you can know beyond a shadow of a doubt. But the truth is that anyone who "knows" God beyond the slightest doubt has little need for faith. We don't need faith in what we "know" to be true. We need faith in what we believe or hope to be true. We have to have faith in that which we cannot prove and which we ourselves sometimes doubt. It is not faith and doubt that are opposites. Rather, it is faith and certainty that are opposites.

We often say that faith is at the center of our lives. Perhaps, reflecting upon the experience of adolescents, we might better speak of faith at the boundaries of life. It doesn't require much faith to stand on the solid ground of my life. Where I really need faith is on the edges, where my balance is insecure. I don't need much faith when I walk the well-worn paths of daily life. I can walk those with my eyes closed. I need faith when I walk with my eyes open and yet still cannot see. I need faith to walk the frontiers where my destination is obscure. It doesn't require as much faith to look at my successes and joys as to face my insecurities and failures.

Faith rarely arises out of a time of feeling adequate about ourselves; those are not the likely times of our conversion. Faith arises, rather, out of our inadequacies, our limits, and our finiteness. Faith relates persons or communities to their limiting boundaries. At the outer limits, faith pushes a person or community to the tension of readiness and growth.

Moses is remembered as a hero of faith, not for staying at home in the wilderness, but for venturing back to Egypt when called. He went forth because God believed in him more than Moses believed in himself. The adolescent pilgrimage takes youth into the unknown and the untried. They must find their way through the process of conversion for the very first time. At one point or another nearly every adolescent stands like Moses at Midian, clinging to the familiar while being called to the creative. Insecurity and self-consciousness are often the name of their game. If that is so, and if faith is most likely to arise from insecurity, then it follows that adolescence is one of life's richest opportunities for developing faith. It is at this point that the role of the courageous evangelist becomes so crucial.

Ministering to Youth at Kairos Time

Ministering to youth at crucial times, in the midst of their insecurities, requires much from those who would be courageous evangelists. As advocates for youth, who we are as persons has a great deal to do with what we offer youth. Successful programs or techniques can never replace the daily witness of our lives, our admissions of doubt, or our supportive friendships with youth. Of course, we are not peers, and we should not act like peers. What youth need from us is friendship with an adult who can serve as advocate and clarifier of their faith. Many youth already have distorted images of adult life. They reflect our cultural distortion of adulthood as a relatively tranquil, settled, linear march to senility and death. The last thing youth need is to be convinced that adults "have it all together." Youth, who are often asking the faith question in terms of trust, need trustworthy adults who struggle along with them in trying to live Christ-worthy lives. They need courageous evangelists. Who we are and how we share our faith journey are more related to evangelism with youth than we might have imagined.

Paul writes to Timothy,

> Do not let people disregard you because you are young, but be an example to all the believers in the way you speak and behave, and in your love, your faith, and your purity. Make use of the time until I arrive by reading to the people, preaching and teaching. You have in you a spiritual gift which was given to you when the prophets spoke and the body of elders laid their hands on you; do not let it lie unused. Think hard about all this, and put it into practice, and everyone will

be able to see how you are advancing (1 Timothy 4:12-15, *The Jerusalem Bible*).

What if young persons today could experience a church that recognizes the gifts of its youth like the early church did with Timothy? What if young persons today had guarantors (like Paul) who insisted that they claim their rightful places and who called forth their gifts for the ministry that was at hand? What if youth today had courageous evangelists like Paul?

Gallup says again from his surveys of youth,

Only as churches recognize youth as meaningful, valid participants, not consumers or some sort of customer to be cultivated, but able and vigorous participants called by God, will we see the possibility of great change and advance for [the church].[2]

The courageous evangelist will not retreat from the hard questions that youth ask nor chase youth away to struggle with these questions on their own. Rather, the courageous evangelist will meet young persons at the church door and say, "Welcome! If you want to work at your salvation, you can work with freedom here. When you point out the contradictions of our faith, when you ask us to look at the great mysteries of life, we will listen with respect. When you must part physically from us for a time, we will still remain a freeing community that cares for you even in the distance. And when you return, in fifteen days or fifteen months or fifteen years, we will celebrate your return, not as a stranger, but as a son or daughter returning home." How easy it would be to turn adolescents *out*—to leave them to struggle on their own. How easy to turn adolescents *off*—by clutching onto them and never giving them freedom to truly explore faith. How courageous is the one who cares enough to stand by the door and say, "Welcome! Let us find Christ through one another. Let us find Christ together."

God's love does not come to youth from out of the clouds. It did not come to us that way. Someone cared enough to share the evangelistic good news. Someone cared enough to tell us that the good news would gradually convert us to think of ourselves as Christ thinks of us. "We love because he [God] loved us first" (John 4:19, NEB).

Jesus once took a young person standing nearby and, drawing him close to his side, said to his disciples—and to all people throughout eternity: "Whoever welcomes in my name one of these young persons into the faith, welcomes me; and whoever welcomes me, welcomes not only me but the one who sent me" (Mark 9:37, paraphrased).

As we welcome young people into the faith, we can experience a conversion through one another. Let us live up to our calling by being courageous evangelists to youth in the church, in the home, and in the youth culture. Young people themselves are reaching for faith, reaching for Christ. Yet they are often trapped in a web of self-consciousness. We have good news for such youth! This is their favorable time, their *kairos* time. This is the day of their salvation!

FOR REFLECTION

1. Identify some of the *kairos* times in your own adolescence and adulthood. Who was helpful to you? In what ways?

2. Identify some *kairos* times in the lives of youth you know. How can you be a courageous evangelist at those particular moments?

3. Brainstorm some specific ways the institutional church can be more intentional and effective in providing the kind of welcome that questioning and questing youth need. How can youth and adults in the church mutually minister to one another through this kind of welcome?

Notes

Chapter 1

[1] Karl Mannheim, "The Problem of Generations," in *Essays on the Sociology of Knowledge,* ed. Paul Kecskemeti (New York: Oxford University Press, Inc., 1952).
[2] Margaret Mead, *Culture and Commitment* (Garden City, N.Y.: Doubleday & Co., Inc., 1970).
[3] Daniel Yankelovich, *New Rules: Searching for Self-Fulfillment in a World Turned Upside Down* (New York: Random House, Inc., 1981), p. 22.
[4] Christopher Lasch, *Haven in a Heartless World: The Family Beseiged* (New York: Basic Books, Inc., Publishers, 1979).
[5] See, for example, Bruce J. Biddle, Barbara J. Bank, and Marjory M. Martin, "Parental and Peer Influence on Adolescents," *Social Forces,* vol. 58, no. 4 (June, 1980), pp. 1057–1079.
[6] Daniel Yankelovich, Inc., and John D. Rockefeller, *Changing Values on Campus: Political and Personal Attitudes of Today's College Students* (New York: Simon & Schuster, Inc., Washington Square Press, 1972), particularly chapter 7.
[7] See Daniel Yankelovich, *A Profile of American Youth in the Seventies* (New York: McGraw-Hill, Inc., 1974).
[8] Erik H. Erikson, *Identity: Youth and Crisis* (New York: W. W. Norton & Co., Inc., 1968), pp. 128–135.

Chapter 2

[1] Daniel Yankelovich, *New Rules: Searching for Self-Fulfillment in a World Turned Upside Down* (New York: Random House, Inc., 1981), pp. 8–10.
[2] Alvin W. Gouldner, *The Future of Intellectuals and the Rise of the New Class* (New York: The Seabury Press, Inc., Continuum Books, 1979), p. 21.

Chapter 3

[1] Erik H. Erikson, *Identity: Youth and Crisis* (New York: W. W. Norton & Co., Inc., 1968), pp. 128–135.
[2] *Ibid.,* pp. 129–130.

[3] Edward A. Wynne, "Behind the Discipline Problem: Youth Suicide as a Measure of Alienation," in the *Phi Delta Kappan,* January 1978, p. 308.

[4] Daniel Yankelovich, *New Rules: Searching for Self-Fulfillment in a World Turned Upside Down* (New York: Random House, Inc., 1981), p. 235.

[5] *Ibid.,* p. 252.

[6] Peter L. Berger, et al., *The Homeless Mind: Modernization and Consciousness* (New York: Random House, Inc., Vintage Books, 1974), p. 27

[7] *Ibid.,* pp. 33-35.

Chapter 4

[1] Peter L. Berger and Richard Neuhaus, *To Empower People: The Role of Mediating Structures in Public Policy* (Washington, D.C.: American Enterprise Institute for Policy Research, 1977).

[2] Alexis de Tocqueville, *Democracy in America,* ed. H. S. Commager, trans. Henry Reeve (New York: Oxford University Press, Inc., 1947), pp. 319-332.

[3] Roger G. Barker, "Ecology and Motivation," *Nebraska Symposium on Motivation,* vol. 8, ed. Marshall R. Jones (Lincoln: University of Nebraska Press, 1960), pp. 1-48.

[4] Eileen Barker, "Who'd Be a Moonie?" in *The Social Impact of New Religious Movements,* ed. Bryan Wilson (Tarrytown, N.Y.: Unification Theological Seminary, Rose of Sharon Press, Inc., 1981).

[5] For a more detailed discussion of these matters, see James B. Nelson, *Moral Nexus: Ethics of Christian Identity and Community* (Philadelphia: The Westminster Press, 1971).

Chapter 5

[1] Thomas Troeger, *Are You Saved? Answers to the Awkward Question* (Philadelphia: The Westminster Press, 1979), p. 16. Copyright © 1979 The Westminster Press. Used by permission.

[2] James W. Fowler, *Stages of Faith: The Psychology of Human Development and the Quest for Meaning* (San Francisco: Harper & Row, Publishers, Inc., 1981), pp. xiii, 14.

[3] R. S. Lee, *Your Growing Child and Religion* (New York: Macmillan, Inc., 1963), p. 208.

[4] John H. Westerhoff III, *Inner Growth–Outer Change: An Educational Guide to Church Renewal* (New York: The Seabury Press, Inc., 1979), p. 5.

Chapter 6

[1] Thomas Troeger, *Are You Saved? Answers to the Awkward Question* (Philadelphia: The Westminster Press, 1979), p. 98. Copyright © 1979 The Westminster Press. Used by permission.

[2] Emilie Griffin, *Turning: Reflections on the Experience of Conversion* (New York: Doubleday & Co., Inc., 1980), p. 15.

[3] George Gallup, Jr., and David Poling, *The Search for America's Faith* (Nashville: Abingdon Press, 1980), p. 48. Copyright © 1980 by Abingdon Press. Used by permission.

[4] John McCall, quoted by Emilie Griffin, *Turning,* p. 23.

[5] Avery Dulles, *A Testimonial to Grace* (Mission, Kans.: Andrews & McMeel, Inc., Sheed and Ward, 1946), p. 118.

[6] C. S. Lewis, *Mere Christianity* (New York: Macmillan, Inc., 1943), p. 86.

[7] Emilie Griffin, *Turning,* p. 157.

[8] Thomas Merton, letter published in *Information Catholiques Internationale,* April 1973, back cover.

[9] John H. Westerhoff III, *Inner Growth–Outer Change: An Educational Guide to Church Renewal* (New York: The Seabury Press, Inc., 1979), p. 15.

[10] Stephen Jones, *Faith Shaping* (Valley Forge: Judson Press, 1980), pp. 27-34.

[11] *Ibid.,* p. 53.

Chapter 7

[1] Wendy Ryan, "Radical Solution/Radical Commitment: World Food Day," *The American Baptist,* vol. 179, no. 8 (September, 1981), p. 13.

[2] Ross Snyder, *Young People and Their Culture* (Nashville: Abingdon Press, 1969), pp. 35-38.

[3] Thomas Troeger, *Are You Saved? Answers to the Awkward Question* (Philadelphia: The Westminster Press, 1979), p. 22. Copyright © 1979 The Westminster Press. Used by permission.

[4] Stephen Jones, *Faith Shaping* (Valley Forge: Judson Press, 1980), p. 44.

[5] George Gallup, Jr., and David Poling, *The Search for America's Faith* (Nashville: Abingdon Press, 1980), p. 35. Copyright © 1980 by Abingdon Press. Used by permission.

Chapter 8

[1] George Gallup, Jr., and David Poling, *The Search for America's Faith* (Nashville: Abingdon Press, 1980), pp. 32-34. Copyright © by Abingdon Press. Used by permission.

[2] *Ibid.,* p. 39.